FORWARD/COMMENTARY

The National Institute of Standards and Technology (NIST) is a measurement standards laboratory, and a non-regulatory agency of the United States Department of Commerce. Its mission is to promote innovation and industrial competitiveness. Founded in 1901, as the National Bureau of Standards, NIST was formed with the mandate to provide standard weights and measures, and to serve as the national physical laboratory for the United States. With a world-class measurement and testing laboratory encompassing a wide range of areas of computer science, mathematics, statistics, and systems engineering, NIST's cybersecurity program supports its overall mission to promote U.S. innovation and industrial competitiveness by advancing measurement science, standards, and related technology through research and development in ways that enhance economic security and improve our quality of life.

The need for cybersecurity standards and best practices that address interoperability, usability and privacy has been shown to be critical for the nation. NIST's cybersecurity programs seek to enable greater development and application of practical, innovative security technologies and methodologies that enhance the country's ability to address current and future computer and information security challenges.

The cybersecurity publications produced by NIST cover a wide range of cybersecurity concepts that are carefully designed to work together to produce a holistic approach to cybersecurity primarily for government agencies and constitute the best practices used by industry. This holistic strategy to cybersecurity covers the gamut of security subjects from development of secure encryption standards for communication and storage of information while at rest to how best to recover from a cyber-attack.

Why buy a book you can download for free?   **We print this so you don't have to.**

Some are available only in electronic media. Some online docs are missing pages or barely legible.

We at 4th Watch Publishing are former government employees, so we know how government employees actually use the standards. When a new standard is released, an engineer prints it out, punches holes and puts it in a 3-ring binder. While this is not a big deal for a 5 or 10-page document, many NIST documents are over 100 pages and printing a large document is a time-consuming effort. So, an engineer that's paid $75 an hour is spending hours simply printing out the tools needed to do the job. That's time that could be better spent doing engineering. We publish these documents so engineers can focus on what they were hired to do – engineering. It's much more cost-effective to just order the latest version from Amazon.com

If there is a standard you would like published, let us know. Our web site is www.usgovpub.com

Many of our titles are available as ePubs for Kindle, iPad, Nook, remarkable, BOOX, and Sony ereaders. Please visit our web site to see our recommendations.

Why buy an eBook when you can access data on a website for free? HYPERLINKS

Yes, many books are available as a PDF, but not all PDFs are bookmarked? Do you really want to search a 6,500-page PDF document manually? Load our copy onto your Kindle, PC, iPad, Android Tablet, Nook, or iPhone (download the FREE kindle App from the APP Store) and you have an easily searchable copy. Most devices will allow you to easily navigate an ePub to any Chapter. Note that there is a distinction between a Table of Contents and "Page Navigation". Page Navigation refers to a different sort of Table of Contents. Not one appearing as a page in the book, but one that shows up on the device itself when the reader accesses the navigation feature. Readers can click on a navigation link to jump to a Chapter or Subchapter. Once there, most devices allow you to "pinch and zoom" in or out to easily read the text. (Unfortunately, downloading the free sample file at Amazon.com does not include this feature. You have to buy a copy to get that functionality, but as inexpensive as eBooks are, it's worth it.) Kindle allows you to do word search and Page Flip (temporary place holder takes you back when you want to go back and check something). Visit **www.usgovpub.com** to learn more.

1
2

Draft NISTIR 8222

3 # Internet of Things (IoT) Trust Concerns

4

5

6 Jeffrey Voas
7 Rick Kuhn
8 Phillip Laplante
9 Sophia Applebaum

10

11

12

13

14

NIST

**National Institute of
Standards and Technology**
U.S. Department of Commerce

Internet of Things (IoT) Trust Concerns

19
20
21
22

Jeffrey Voas
Rick Kuhn
Computer Security Division
Information Technology Laboratory

23
24
25
26

Phillip Laplante
Penn State

27
28
29
30

Sophia Applebaum
Mobile and Emerging Technology
The MITRE Corporation
McLean, Virginia

31
32
33
34
35
36

September 2018

37
38

39
40
41
42
43

U.S. Department of Commerce
Wilbur L. Ross, Jr., Secretary

44
45
46

National Institute of Standards and Technology
Walter Copan, NIST Director and Under Secretary of Commerce for Standards and Technology

47 National Institute of Standards and Technology Internal Report 8222
48 56 pages (September 2018)
49

50

64

65 **Public comment period: *September 17, 2018* through *November 5, 2018***

66 National Institute of Standards and Technology
67 Attn: Computer Security Division, Information Technology Laboratory
68 100 Bureau Drive (Mail Stop 8930) Gaithersburg, MD 20899-8930
69 Email: iot@nist.gov

70 All comments are subject to release under the Freedom of Information Act (FOIA).

71   **Reports on Computer Systems Technology**

72   The Information Technology Laboratory (ITL) at the National Institute of Standards and
73   Technology (NIST) promotes the U.S. economy and public welfare by providing technical
74   leadership for the Nation's measurement and standards infrastructure. ITL develops tests, test
75   methods, reference data, proof of concept implementations, and technical analyses to advance the
76   development and productive use of information technology. ITL's responsibilities include the
77   development of management, administrative, technical, and physical standards and guidelines for
78   the cost-effective security and privacy of other than national security-related information in federal
79   information systems.

80   **Abstract**

81   The Internet of Things (IoT) refers to systems that involve computation, sensing, communication,
82   and actuation (as presented in NIST Special Publication (SP) 800-183). IoT involves the
83   connection between humans, non-human physical objects, and cyber objects, enabling monitoring,
84   automation, and decision making. The connection is complex and inherits a core set of trust
85   concerns, most of which have no current resolution This publication identifies 17 technical trust-
86   related concerns for individuals and organizations before and after IoT adoption. The set of
87   concerns discussed here is necessarily incomplete given this rapidly changing industry, however
88   this publication should still leave readers with a broader understanding of the topic. This set was
89   derived from the six trustworthiness elements in NIST SP 800-183. And when possible, this
90   publication outlines recommendations for how to mitigate or reduce the effects of these IoT
91   concerns. It also recommends new areas of IoT research and study. This publication is intended
92   for a general information technology audience including managers, supervisors, technical staff,
93   and those involved in IoT policy decisions, governance, and procurement.

94   **Keywords**

95   Internet of Things (IoT); computer security; trust; confidence; network of 'things';
96   interoperability; scalability; reliability; testing; environment; standards; measurement;
97   timestamping; algorithms; software testing

98

99   **Acknowledgments**

100   Appreciation is given to Dave Ferraiolo for encouragement to author this publication.
101   Appreciation is also given to Matt Scholl for his continuous support of this IoT research in the
102   Computer Security Division over the past 4 years.

103   **Note to Reviewers**

104   The authors request that reviewers provide feedback on the 17 technical concerns that are
105   presented in this publication and suggest other potential technical concerns that they feel are
106   missing from the document.

107
108 **Executive Summary**

109   The Internet of Things (IoT) is utilized in almost every aspect of personal life and is being
110   adopted within nearly every industry. Governments are taking notice and are looking at IoT from
111   a variety of dimensions. One dimension is how IoT systems can improve efficiency, analytics,
112   intelligence, and decision making. Another dimension deals with regulation, i.e., is IoT a
113   technology that needs governance, legislation, and standards due to its universal reach and
114   impact? For example, IoT carries security concerns due to its high degree of connectivity. Should
115   there be rules or laws specific to IoT security issues? And the same applies to privacy, safety,
116   and dependability.

117   As with any new, unproven technology, questions about trustworthiness arise. Those questions
118   often boil down to this: are the benefits worth the risks, i.e., are there more positive reasons to
119   adopt a new technology than to avoid it? If answered with 'yes', a secondary question is: how
120   can you minimize the risks to make the technology more acceptable and therefore 'suitable for
121   use' by a wider audience? Most new technologies are created to benefit humanity, however those
122   technologies in the wrong hands can enable new and unforeseen nefarious actions.

123   This publication is not directly focused on risk assessment and risk mitigation, but instead on
124   trust. That is, will an IoT product or service provide the desired operations with an acceptable
125   level of quality? To answer this question, the analysis begins with a simple understanding of
126   trust. Here, trust is the probability that the *intended* behavior and the *actual* behavior are
127   equivalent, given a fixed context, fixed environment, and fixed point in time. Trust is viewed as a
128   *level of confidence*. In this publication, trust is considered at two levels: (1) can a 'thing' or
129   device trust the data it receives, and (2) can a human trust the 'things', services, data, or
130   complete IoT offerings that it uses. This document focuses more on the human trust concern
131   than the concern of 'things' to trust data (however both are important).

132   This publication promotes awareness of 17 technical concerns that can negatively affect one's
133   ability to trust IoT products and services. It is intended for a general information technology
134   audience including managers, supervisors, technical staff, and those involved in IoT policy
135   decisions, governance, and procurement. This publication should be of interest to early adopters
136   and persons responsible for integrating the various devices and services into purposed IoT
137   offerings. The following is a brief synopsis of each technical concern.

138   **Scalability**

139   This trust concern occurs from a combinatorial explosion in the number of 'things' that are part
140   of a system. 'Things', and the services to interconnect them are often relatively inexpensive
141   therefore creating an opportunity for functionality bloat. This allows complexity to skyrocket
142   causing difficulty for testing, security, and performance. If the average person is associated with
143   10 or more IoT 'things', the number of 'things' requiring connectivity explodes quickly and so
144   do bandwidth and energy demands. Combinatorial explosion and functionality bloat are trust
145   concerns.

146   **Heterogeneity**

147   This trust concern results from competition in the marketplace. The argument goes that with
148   more choices, the competition will result in lower prices. While true, the ability of heterogeneous
149   'things' to interoperate and integrate creates a different tension related to emergent behaviors.
150   And heterogeneity will almost definitely create *emergent behaviors* that will enable new and
151   unknown security vulnerabilities as well as impact other concerns such as reliability and
152   performance. Potential vulnerability issues related to heterogeneity also occur with *supply chain*
153   applications.

154   **Ownership and Control**

155   This trust concern occurs when much of the functionality within an IoT system originates from
156   third party vendors. Third party black-box devices make trust more difficult for integrators and
157   adopters to assess. This is particularly true for security and reliability since the internal
158   'workings' of black-boxes are not observable and transparent. No internal computations can be
159   specifically singled out and individually tested. Black-box 'things' can contain malicious trojan
160   behaviors. When IoT adopters better understand the magnitude of losing access to the internals
161   of these acquired functions, they will recognize limitations to trust in their composite IoT
162   systems.

163   **Composability, Interoperability, Integration, and Compatibility**

164   This trust concern occurs because hardware and software components may not work well when
165   composed, depending on whether: (1) the "right" components were selected, (2) the components
166   had the proper security and reliability built-in, and (3) the architecture and specification of the
167   system that the components will be incorporated into was correct. Further, problems arise if
168   components cannot be swapped in or out to satisfy system requirements, components cannot
169   communicate, and components cannot work in conjunction without conflict. Integration,
170   interoperability, compatibility, and composability each impact IoT trust in a slightly different
171   manner for networks of 'things', and each 'thing' should be evaluated before adoption into a
172   system for each of these four properties.

173   **"Ilities"**

174   This trust concern deals with the *quality* attributes frequently referred to as "ilities. Functional
175   requirements state what a system *shall* do. Negative requirements state what a system *shall not*
176   do, and non-functional requirements, i.e., the "ilities", typically state what *level of quality* the
177   system shall exhibit both for the functional and negative requirements. One difficulty for IoT
178   adopters and integrators is that there are dozens of "ilities" and most are not easily measured.
179   Another difficulty is that technically a system cannot have high levels of all "ilities" since some
180   are in technical conflict. For example, higher security typically means lower performance. And
181   finally, deciding which "ilities" are more important and at what level and cost is not a well
182   understood process. No cookbook approach exists. So, although quality is desired, getting it is
183   the challenge.

184   **Synchronization**

185   This trust concern stems from IoT systems being distributed computing systems. Distributed
186   computing systems have different computations and events occurring concurrently. There can be
187   numerous computations and events (e.g., data transfers) occurring in parallel and those
188   computations and events must need some degree of synchronization. For that to occur, a timing
189   mechanism is needed that applies to all computations and events, however no such global clock
190   exists. Therefore, timing anomalies will occur, enabling vulnerabilities, poor performance, and
191   IoT failures.

192   **Measurement**

193   This trust concern stems from a lack of IoT metrics and measures. Metrics and measures are
194   keystones of trust. Since IoT is a relatively young set of technologies, few metrics and measures
195   are available to adopters and integrators. To date, there are few ways to measure IoT systems
196   other than by *counting* 'things' or dynamic testing. Because of this, it becomes difficult to argue
197   that a system is trustable or even estimate the amount of testing that a system should receive.

198   **Predictability**

199   This trust concern stems from an inability to predict how different components will interact. The
200   ability to design useful IT systems depends at a fundamental level on predictability, the
201   assurance that components will provide the resources, performance, and functions that are
202   specified when they are needed. This is hard enough to establish in a conventional system, but
203   an extensive body of knowledge in queueing theory and related subjects has been developed.
204   IoT systems will provide an even greater challenge, since more components will interact in
205   different ways, and possibly not at consistent times.

206   **Testing and Assurance**

207   This trust concern stems from the additional testing challenges created by IoT beyond those
208   encountered with conventional systems. The numerous number of interdependencies alone create
209   testing difficulty because of the large numbers of tests that are needed to simply cover some
210   percentage of the interdependencies. Testing concerns always increase when devices and
211   services are black-box and offer no transparency into their internal "workings." Most IoT
212   systems will be built from only black-box devices and services. Also, IoT systems are highly
213   data-driven, and assuring the integrity of the data and assuring that a system is resilient to data
214   anomalies will be required. These are just a few of the many testing and assurance problems
215   related to IoT.

216   **Certification**

217   This trust concern occurs because certification is difficult and often causes conflict. Questions
218   immediately arise as to what criteria will be selected, and who will perform the certification.
219   Other questions that arise include: (1) What is the impact on time-to-market if the system
220   undergoes certification prior to operation? (2) What is the lifespan of a 'thing' relative to the
221   time required to certify that 'thing'? and (3) What is the value of building a system from 'things'

222   of which very few received certification? Without acceptable answers to such questions it is
223   unlikely that certification can offer the degree of trust most IoT adopters would want.

Security

225   Security is a trust concern for all 'things' in IoT systems. For example, sensors data may be
226   tampered with, stolen, deleted, dropped, or transmitted insecurely allowing it to be accessed by
227   unauthorized parties. IoT devices may be counterfeited and default credentials are still widely
228   used. Further, unlike traditional personal computers, there are few security upgrade processes for
229   'things' such as patches and updates.

Reliability

231   Reliability is a trust concern for all IoT systems and 'things.' It will rarely be possible to claim
232   that an IoT system works perfectly for any environment, context, and for any anomalous event
233   that the system can experience. What this means for trust is that reliability assessments depend
234   heavily on correct knowledge of the context and environment and resilience to handle anomalous
235   events and data. Rarely will such knowledge exist and provide complete resilience.

Data Integrity

237   This trust concern focuses on the quality of the data that is generated by or fed into an IoT
238   system. The quality of the data flowing between devices and from sensors will directly impact
239   whether an IoT system is fit-for-purpose. Data is the 'blood' flowing through IoT systems. The
240   ability to trust data involves many factors: (1) accuracy, (2) fidelity, (3) availability, (4)
241   confidence that the data cannot be corrupted or tampered with, etc. Cloud computing epitomizes
242   the importance of trusting data. Where data resides is important. Where is the cloud? And can
243   the data be leaked from that location? It is a tendency to think of "your data" on "your machine."
244   But in some cases, the data is not just "yours." Leased data can originate from anywhere and
245   from vendors at the time of their choosing and with the integrity of their choosing. These trust
246   concerns should be considered during IoT system development and throughout operation.

Excessive data

248   This trust concern is overwhelming amounts of data that that gets generated and is processed in
249   an IoT system. IoT systems are likely to have a dynamic and rapidly changing dataflow and
250   workflow. There may be numerous inputs from a variety of sources such as sensors, external
251   databases or clouds, and other external subsystems. The potential for the generation of vast
252   amounts of data over time renders IoT systems as potential 'big data' generators. The possibly of
253   not being able to guarantee the integrity of excessive amounts of data or even process that data is
254   a trustworthiness concern.

Performance

256   This trust concern is too much performance. This may seem counterintuitive. The speed at which
257   computations and data generation can occur in an IoT system is increasing rapidly. Increased
258   computational speed inhibits a systems' ability to log and audit any transactions as the rate of
259   data generation exceeds the speed of storage. This situation, in turn, makes real-time forensic

260   analysis and recovery from faults and failures more difficult as data is lost and computational
261   deadlines become harder to meet. Consequently, there are fewer ways to "put on the brakes,"
262   undo incorrect computations, and fix internal and external data anomalies. Furthermore,
263   computing faster to a wrong outcome offers little trust.

264   **Usability**

265   This trust concern deals with whether users understand how to use the devices that that they have
266   access to. How "friendly" are IoT devices to use and learn? This quality is an important
267   consideration for most IT systems, but may be more of a challenge with IoT, where the user
268   interface may be tightly constrained by limited display size and functionality, or where a device
269   can only be controlled via remote means. User interfaces for some device classes, such as Smart
270   Home devices, are often limited to a small set of onboard features (e.g., LED status indicators
271   and a few buttons) and a broader set of display and control parameters accessible remotely via a
272   computer or mobile device. Usability and other trust concerns to which usability is intimately
273   tied have significant implications for user trust.

274   **Visibility and Discovery**

275   The visibility trust concern manifests when technologies become so ingrained into daily life that
276   they disappear from users. If you cannot see a technology, how do you know what else it might
277   be doing? For example, with voice response technology such as a smart speaker, when you talk
278   to the device, do you know if it is the only system listening, and do you know if the sounds that it
279   hears are stored somewhere for eternity and linked to you?

280   The discovery trust concern stems from the fact that the traditional internet was built almost
281   entirely on the TCP/IP protocol suite, with HTML for web sites running on top of TCP/IP.
282   Standardized communication port numbers and internationally agreed web domain names
283   enabled consistent operation regardless of the computer or router manufacturer. This structure
284   has not extended to IoT devices, because they generally do not have the processing power to
285   support it. This has enabled many new protocol families causing a vast number of possible
286   interactions among various versions of software and hardware from many different sources.
287   These interactions are prone to security and reliability problems.

288   In addition to these the 17 concerns, this publication concludes with 2 non-technical, trust-related
289   appendices. Appendix A reviews the impact that many of the 17 technical concerns have on
290   insurability and risk measurement. Appendix B discusses how a lack of IoT regulatory oversight
291   and governance affects users of IoT technologies by creating a vacuum of trust in the products
292   and services that they can access.

293

294

295   **Table of Contents**

320

321   **List of Appendices**

327

328 **1   Introduction**

329   The Internet of Things (IoT) is being utilized in almost every aspect of life today, although this
330   fact is often unknown and not advertised. The incorporation of IoT into everyday processes will
331   continue to increase.

332   According to Forbes magazine [Columbus, 2017] there will be a significant increase in spending
333   on the design and development of IoT applications and analytics. Furthermore, the biggest
334   increases will be in the business-to-business (b2b) IoT systems (e.g. manufacturing, healthcare,
335   agriculture, transportation, utilities etc.), which will reach $267B by 2020. In addition to b2b,
336   smart products are becoming more prevalent such as smart homes, smart cars, smart TVs, even
337   smart light bulbs and other basic commodities. In other words, products that can sense, learn,
338   and react to user preferences are gaining acceptance and are deployed in modern living.

339   The term Internet of Things" (IoT) is a metaphor that was coined by Kevin Ashton in 1999
340   [Ashton, 2009] although he prefers the phrase "Internet *for* things" [BBC, 2016]. IoT is an
341   acronym comprised of three letters: (I), (o), and (T). The (o) matters little, and as already
342   mentioned, 'of' might be better replaced by 'for.' The Internet (I) existed long before the IoT
343   acronym was coined, and so it is the 'things' (T) that makes IoT different from previous IT
344   systems and computing approaches. 'Things' are what make IoT unique. Many people question
345   whether IoT is just marketing hype or is there a science behind it. That's a fair question to ask
346   about any new, unproven technology.

347   The acronym IoT currently has no universally-accepted and actionable definition. However,
348   attempts have been made. A few examples include:

349   • *"The term Internet of Things generally refers to scenarios where network connectivity*
350   *and computing capability extends to objects, sensors and everyday items not normally*
351   *considered computers, allowing these devices to generate, exchange and consume data*
352   *with minimal human intervention."* The Internet of Things (IoT): An Overview, Karen
353   Rose, et.al. The Internet Society, October 2015. p. 5.

354   • *"Although there is no single definition for the Internet of Things, competing visions agree*
355   *that it relates to the integration of the physical world with the virtual world – with any*
356   *object having the potential to be connected to the Internet via short-range wireless*
357   *technologies, such as radio frequency identification (RFID), near field communication*
358   *(NFC), or wireless sensor networks (WSNs). This merging of the physical and virtual*
359   *worlds is intended to increase instrumentation, tracking, and measurement of both*
360   *natural and social processes."* "Algorithmic Discrimination: Big Data Analytics and the
361   Future of the Internet", Jenifer Winter. In: *The Future Internet: Alternative Visions.*
362   Jenifer Winter and Ryota Ono, eds. Springer, December 2015. p. 127.

363   • *"The concept of Internet of Things (IOT) ... is that every object in the Internet*
364   *infrastructure is interconnected into a global dynamic expanding network."* "An efficient
365   user authentication and key agreement scheme for heterogeneous wireless sensor network

366   tailored for the Internet of Things environment", Mohammad Sabzinejad Farasha, et.al.
367   *Ad Hoc Networks* 36(1), January 2016.

368   Instead of offering an official definition of IoT in 2016, NIST published a document titled
369   "Networks of 'Things'" to partially address the deficit of having an accepted IoT definition
370   [NIST, 2016]. In that document, five primitives were presented that can be visualized as
371   Lego™-like building blocks for any network of 'things.' The primitives are the (T)s.

372   The primitives are: (1) sensors (*a physical utility that measures physical properties*), (2)
373   aggregators (*software that transforms big data into smaller data*), (3) communication channels
374   (*data transmission utilities that allows 'things' to communicate with 'things'*), (4) *e*-Utilities
375   (*software or hardware components that perform computation*), and a (5) decision trigger (*an
376   algorithm and implementation that satisfies the purpose of a network of 'things' by creating the
377   final output*). Note that any purposed network of 'things' may not include all five. For example,
378   a network of 'things' can exist without sensors. And note that having a model of the components
379   of a network of 'things' is still not a definition of IoT.

380   Before leaving the problem of having no universally accepted and actionable definition for IoT,
381   it should be stated that IoT is increasingly associated with Artificial Intelligence (AI),
382   automation, and 'smart' objects. So, is "IoT" any *noun* you can attach the adjective "smart" onto,
383   e.g., smart phone, smart car, smart appliance, smart toy, smart home, smart watch, smart grid,
384   smart city, smart tv, smart suitcase, smart clothes, etc.? No answer is offered here, but it is
385   something to consider, because the overuse of the adjective 'smart' adds confusion as to what
386   IoT is about.

387   Now consider the question: what is meant by 'trust?' No formal definition is suggested in this
388   publication, but rather a variation on the classical definition of reliability. Here, trust is the
389   probability that the *intended* behavior and the *actual* behavior are equivalent, given a fixed
390   context, fixed environment, and fixed point in time. Trust should be viewed as a *level of
391   confidence*. For example, cars have a trusted set of behaviors when operating on a roadway. The
392   same set of behaviors cannot be expected when the car is sunken in a lake. This informal trust
393   definition works well when discussing both 'things' and networks of 'things'.

394   The value of knowing intended behaviors cannot be dismissed when attempting to establish trust.
395   Lack of access to a specification for intended behaviors is a trust concern. Even if there is little
396   difficulty gluing 'things' to other 'things', that still only addresses a network of 'things'
397   architecture and that is one piece of determining trust. Correct architecture does not ensure that
398   the actual behavior of the composed 'things' will exhibit the intended composite behavior.
399   Hardware and software components may not work well when integrated, depending on whether
400   they were the right components to be selected, whether they had the proper levels of "ilities"
401   such as security and reliability built-in, and whether the architecture and specification for the
402   composition was correct.

403   The Internet (I) is rarely associated with the term 'trust' or 'trustable.' Identity theft, false
404   information, the dark web, breakdown in personal privacy, and other negative features of (I)
405   have caused some people to avoid the Internet altogether. But for most, avoidance is not an
406   option. Similar trust concerns occur for (T) because 'things' carry their own trust concerns and

407   the interactions between 'things' can exacerbate these concerns. From a trust standpoint, the
408   Internet should be viewed as an untrustworthy backbone with untrustworthy things attached –
409   that becomes a perfect storm. Hence, there are three categories of IoT trust that must be
410   addressed: (1) trust in a 'thing', (2) trust in a network of 'things', and (3) trust that the
411   environment and context that the network will operate in is known and the network will be *fit for*
412   *purpose* in that environment, context, and at a specific point in time.

413   Understanding what IoT is and what trust means is the first step in confidently relying on IoT.
414   IoT is a complex, distributed system with temporal constraints. This publication highlights 17
415   technical concerns that should be considered before and after deploying IoT systems. This set
416   has been derived from the six trustworthiness elements presented in NIST SP 800-183 (the six
417   are reprinted in Appendix C.)

418   The 17 technical concerns are: (1) scalability, (2) heterogeneity, (3) control and ownership, (4)
419   composability, interoperability, integration, and compatibility, (5) "ilities", (6) synchronization,
420   (7) measurement, (8) predictability, (9) IoT-specific testing and assurance approaches, (10) IoT
421   certification criteria, (11) security, (12) reliability, (13) data integrity, (14) excessive data, (15)
422   speed and performance, (16) usability, and (17) visibility and discovery. The publication also
423   offers recommendations for ways to reduce the impacts of some of the 17 concerns.

424   This publication also addresses two non-technical trust concerns in Appendix A and Appendix B.
425   Appendix A discusses insurability and risk measurement, and Appendix B discusses a lack of
426   regulatory oversight and governance.

427   In summary, this document advances the original six IoT trust elements presented in [NIST,
428   2016]. This document also serves as a roadmap for where new research and thought leadership is
429   needed. This publication is intended for a general audience including managers, supervisors,
430   technical staff, and those involved in IoT policy decisions, governance, and procurement.

431

432 ## 2   Overwhelming Scalability

433 Computing is now embedded in products as mundane as lightbulbs and kitchen faucets. When
434 computing becomes part of the tiniest of consumer products, scalability quickly becomes an
435 issue, particularly if these products require network connectivity. Referring back to the
436 primitives introduced earlier, scalability issues are seen particularly with the sensors and
437 aggregators components of IoT. Collecting and aggregating data from 10s to 100s of devices
438 sensing their environment can quickly become a performance issue.

439 Consider this analysis. If the average person is associated with 10 or more IoT 'things', the
440 number of 'things' requiring connectivity explodes quickly and so do bandwidth and energy
441 demands. Therefore computing, architecture, and verification changes are inevitable, particularly
442 if predictions of 20 billion to 50 billion new IoT devices being created within the next three years
443 come true. More 'things' will require a means of communication between the 'things' and the
444 consumers they serve, and the need for inter-communication between 'things' adds an additional
445 scalability concern beyond simply counting the number of 'things' [Voas, 2018a].

446 Increased scalability leads to increased complexity. Note that although increased scalability leads
447 to complexity, the converse is not necessarily true. Increased complexity can arise from other
448 factors such as infinite numbers of dataflows and workflows.

449 Unfortunately, complexity does not lend itself to trust that is easy to verify. Consider an
450 analogous difficulty that occurs during software testing when the number of Source Lines of
451 Code (SLOC) increases. Generally, when SLOC increases, more test cases are needed to achieve
452 greater testing coverage.[1] Simple statement testing coverage is the process of making sure that
453 there exists a test case that touches (executes) each line of code during test. As SLOC increases,
454 so may the number of paths though the code, and when conditional statements are considered,
455 the number of test cases to exercise all of them thoroughly (depending on the definition of
456 thoroughness) becomes combinatorically explosive.[2] IoT systems will likely suffer from a
457 similar scalability concern that will impact their ability to have trust verified via testing.

458 Thus, IoT systems will likely suffer from a similar combinatorial explosion to that just
459 mentioned for source code paths. The number of potential dataflow and workflow paths for a
460 network of 'things' with feedback loops becomes intractable quickly, thus leading to a
461 combinatorial explosion that impacts the ability to test with any degree of thoroughness. This is
462 due to the expense in time and money. Further, just as occurs in software code testing, finding

---

[1] This difficulty does not occur for straight-line code that contains no branches or jumps, which is rare.

[2] There are software coverage testing techniques to address testing paths and exercising complex conditional expressions,
    however for these more complex forms of software testing coverage, the ability to generate appropriate test cases can
    become infeasible due to a lack of reachability, i.e., is there any test case in the universe that can execute this scenario?

463   test scenarios to exercise many of the paths will not be feasible.[3] IoT testing concerns are
464   discussed further in Section 10.

465   In summary, avoiding the inevitable concern of large scale for many IoT systems will not be
466   practical. However, a network of 'things' can have bounds placed on it, e.g., limiting access to
467   the Internet. By doing such, the threat space for a specific network of 'things' is reduced, and
468   testing becomes more tractable and thorough. And by considering sub-networks of 'things',
469   divide-and-conquer trust approaches can be devised that at least offer trust to higher level
470   components than simple 'things.'

471

---

[3] This is the classic test case generation dilemma, i.e., what can you do when you cannot find the type of test case you need?

3   Heterogeneity

472

473   The heterogeneity of 'things' is economically desirable because it fosters marketplace
474   competition. But today, IoT creates technical problems that mirror past problems when various
475   flavors of Unix and Postscript did not interoperate, integrate, or compose well. Then, different
476   versions of Postscript might or might not print on a specific printer and moving Unix
477   applications to different Unix platforms did not necessarily mean the applications would execute.
478   It was common to ask which "flavor of Unix" would a vendor's product operate on.

479   As with scalability, issues concerning heterogeneity are inevitable as IoT networks are
480   developed. A network of 'things' is simply a system of 'things' that are made by various
481   manufacturers and these 'things' will have certain tolerances (or intolerances) to the other
482   'things' that they are connected to and communicate with.

483   The marketplace of 'things' and services (e.g., wireless communication protocols and clouds)
484   will allow for the architecture of IoT offerings with functionality from multiple vendors. Ideally,
485   the architecture for a network of 'things' will allow IoT products and services to be swapped in
486   and out quickly but often that will not be the case.

487   Heterogeneity will create problems in getting 'things' to integrate and interoperate with other
488   'things', particularly when they are from different and often competing vendors, and these issues
489   must be considered for all five classes of IoT primitives [NIST, 2016]. This is discussed more in
490   Section 5. And heterogeneity will almost definitely create *emergent behaviors* that will enable
491   new and unknown security vulnerabilities as well as impact other concerns such as reliability and
492   performance.

493   And finally, this is an appropriate place to mention potential vulnerability issues related to *supply*
494   *chain*. For example, how do you know that a particular 'thing' is not counterfeit? Do you know
495   where the 'thing' originated from? Do you trust any documentation related to the specification of
496   a 'thing' or warranties of how the 'thing' was tested by the manufacturer? While supply chain is
497   a concern that is too large to dwell on here with any depth, a simple principle does appear: as
498   heterogeneity increases, it is likely that supply chain concerns will also increase.

499

500 ┃ **4   Loss of Ownership and Control**

501   Third party black-box devices make trust more difficult for integrators and adopters to assess.
502   This is particularly true for security and reliability in networks of 'things.' When a 'thing' is a
503   black-box, the internals of the 'thing' are not visible. No internal computations can be
504   specifically singled out and individually tested. Black-box 'things' can contain malicious trojan
505   behaviors. Black-boxes have no transparency.

506   Long-standing black-box software reliability testing approaches are a prior example of how to
507   view this dilemma. In black-box software reliability testing, the software under test is viewed
508   strictly by (input, output) pairs. There, the best that can be done is to build tables of (input,
509   output) pairs, and if the tables become large enough, they can offer hints about the functionality
510   of the box and its internals. This process becomes an informal means to attempt to reverse
511   engineer functionality. In contrast, when source code is available, white-box testing approaches
512   can be applied. White-box software testing offers internal visibility to the lower-level
513   computations (e.g., at the line-of-code level).

514   This testing approach is particularly important for networks of 'things.' It is likely that most of
515   the physical 'things' that will be employed in a network of 'things' will be 3rd party, commercial,
516   and therefore are commercial off-the-shelf (COTS). Therefore, visibility into the inner workings
517   of a network of 'things' may only be possible at the communication interface layer [Voas, 1996].

518   Consider the following scenario: A hacked refrigerator's software interacts with an app on a
519   person's smartphone, installing a security exploit that can be propagated to other applications
520   with which the phone interacts. The user enters their automobile and their phone interacts with
521   the vehicle's operator interface software, which downloads the new software, including the
522   defect. Unfortunately, the software defect causes an interaction problem (e.g., a deadlock) that
523   leads to a failure in the software-controlled safety system during a crash, leading to injury. A
524   scenario such as this is sometimes referred to as a *chain of custody*.

525   The above scenario demonstrates how losing control of the cascading events during operation
526   can result in failure. This sequence also illustrates the challenge of identifying and mitigating
527   interdependency risks and assigning blame when something goes wrong (using techniques such
528   as propagation analysis and traceability analysis). And liability claims are hard to win since the
529   "I agree to all terms" button is usually non-avoidable [Voas, 2017a]. (See Section 13.)

530   Public clouds are important for implementing the economic benefits of IoT. Public clouds are
531   black-box services. Public clouds are a commercial commodity where vendors rely on service-
532   level agreements for legal protection from security problems and other forms of inferior service
533   form their offerings. Integrators and adopters have few protections here. Further, what properties
534   associated with trust can integrators and adopters test for in public clouds?

535   There are examples of where an organization might be able to test for some aspects of trust in a
536   public cloud: (1) performance (i.e., latency time to retrieve data and the computational time to
537   execute a software app or algorithm), and (2) data leakage. Performance is a more
538   straightforward measure to assess using traditional performance testing approaches. Data leakage
539   is harder, but not impossible. By storing data that, if leaked, is easy to detect, i.e., credit card

540 information, a bank can quickly notify a card owner when an illegitimate transaction was
541 attempted. Note, however, such tests that do not result in the observation of leakage do not prove
542 that a cloud is not leaking since such testing does not guarantee complete observability and is not
543 exhaustive. This is no different than the traditional software testing problem where 10 successive
544 passing tests (meaning that no failures were observed) does not guarantee that the 11th test will
545 also be successful.

546 In summary, concerns related to loss of ownership and control are often human, legal, and
547 contractual. Technical recommendations cannot fully address these. It should be mentioned,
548 though, that these concerns can be enumerated (e.g., as misuse or abuse cases) and evaluated
549 during risk assessments and risk mitigation in the design and specification phases of a network of
550 'things.' And this risk assessment and risk mitigation may, and possibly should, continue
551 throughout operation and deployment.

552

5   Composability, Interoperability, Integration, and Compatibility

553

554   Hardware and software components may not work well when composed, depending on whether:
555   (1) the "right" components were selected, (2) the components had the proper security and
556   reliability built-in (as well as other quality attributes), and (3) the architecture and specification
557   of the system that the components will be incorporated into was correct.

558   Note there is a subtle difference between composability, interoperability, integration, and
559   compatibility. *Composability* addresses the issue of sub-systems and components and the degree
560   to which a sub-system or component can be swapped in or out to satisfy a system's requirements.
561   *Interoperability* occurs at the interface level, meaning that when interfaces are understood, two
562   distinct sub-systems can communicate via a common communication format without needing
563   knowledge concerning the functionality of the sub-systems. *Integration* is a process of often
564   bringing together disparate sub-systems into a new system. And *compatibility* simply means that
565   two sub-systems can exist or work in conjunction without conflict.

566   Integration, interoperability, compatibility, and composability each impact IoT trust in a slightly
567   different manner for networks of 'things', and each 'thing' should be evaluated before adoption
568   into a system for each of these four properties.

569   Consider previous decades of building *Systems of Systems* (SoS). Engineering systems from
570   smaller components is nothing new. This engineering principle is basic and taught in all
571   engineering disciplines and building networks of 'things' should be no different. However, this is
572   where IoT's concerns of heterogeneity, scalability, and a lack of ownership and control converge
573   to differentiate traditional SoS engineering from IoT composition.

574   Consider military-critical and safety-critical systems. Such systems require components that have
575   prescriptive requirements. The systems themselves will also have prescriptive architectures that
576   require that each component's specification is considered before adoption. Having access to
577   information concerning the functionality, results from prior testing, and expected usage of
578   components are always required before building critical systems.

579   IoT systems will likely not have these prescriptive capabilities. IoT's 'things' may or may not
580   even have specifications, and the system being built may not have a complete or formal
581   specification. It may be more of an informal definition of what the system is to do, but without
582   an architecture for how the system should be built. Depending on: (1) the grade of a system (e.g.,
583   consumer, industrial, military, etc.), (2) the criticality (e.g., safety-critical, business-critical, life-
584   critical, security-critical, etc.), and (3) the domain (e.g., healthcare financial, agricultural,
585   transportation, entertainment, energy, etc.), the level of effort required to specify and build an
586   IoT system can be approximated. However, no cookbook-like guidance yet exists.

587   In summary, specific recommendations for addressing the inevitable issues of composability,
588   interoperability, integration, and compatibility are: (1) understand the actual behaviors of the
589   'things', (2) understand the environment, context, and timing that each 'thing' will operate in, (3)
590   understand the communication channels between the 'things' [NIST, 2016], (4) apply systems of
591   systems design and architecture principles when applicable, (5) and apply the appropriate risk

592   assessment and risk mitigation approaches during architecture and design based on the grade,
593   criticality, and domain.

594

595 | **6   Abundance of "Ilities"**

596 A trust concern for networks of 'things' deals with the *quality* attributes termed "ilities" [Voas,
597 2004]. Functional requirements state what a system *shall* do. Negative requirements state what a
598 system *shall not* do, and non-functional requirements, i.e., the "ilities" typically state what *level of*
599 *quality* the system shall exhibit both for the functional and negative requirements. "Ilities" apply
600 to both 'things' and the systems they are built into.

601 It is unclear how many "ilities" there are – it depends on who you ask. This document mentions
602 each of these "ilities" in various contexts and level of detail: availability, composability,
603 compatibility, dependability, discoverability, durability, fault tolerance, flexibility,
604 interoperability, insurability, liability, maintainability, observability, privacy, performance,
605 portability, predictability, probability of failure, readability, reliability, resilience, reachability,
606 safety, scalability, security, sustainability, testability, traceability, usability, visibility,
607 vulnerability. Most of these will apply to 'things' and networks of 'things.' However, not all
608 readers will consider all of these to be legitimate "ilities."

609 One difficulty here is that for some "ilities" there is a subsumes hierarchy. For example, reliability,
610 security, privacy, performance, and resilience are "ilities" that are grouped into what LaPrie et. al
611 termed as *dependability*[4]. While having a subsumes hierarchy might appear to simply the
612 relationship between different "ilities", that is not necessarily the case. This can create confusion.

613 Building levels of the "ilities" into a network of 'things' is costly and not all "ilities" cooperate
614 with each other, i.e., "building in" more security can reduce performance [Voas, 2015]. Another
615 example would be fault tolerance and testability. Fault-tolerant systems are designed to mask
616 errors during operation. Testable systems are those that do not mask errors and make it easier for
617 a test case to notify when something is in error inside of a system. Deciding which "ilities" are
618 more important is difficult from both a cost-benefit trade-off analysis and a technical trade-off
619 analysis. Also, some "ilities" can be quantified and others cannot. For those that cannot be
620 quantified, qualified measures exist.

621 Further, consider an "ility" such as reliability. Reliability can be assessed for: (1) a 'thing', (2)
622 the interfaces between 'things', and (3) the network of 'things itself [Voas, 1997]. And these
623 three types of assessments apply to most "ilities."

624 Deciding which "ilities" are more important and at what level and cost is not a well understood
625 process. No cookbook approach exists. The point here is that these non-functional requirements
626 often play just as important of a role in terms of the overall system quality as do functional
627 requirements. This reality will impact the satisfaction of the integrators and adopters with the
628 resulting network.

---

[4] From Wikipedia: In systems engineering, **dependability** is a measure of a system's **availability**, **reliability**, and its **maintainability**, and **maintenance support performance**, and, in some cases, other characteristics such as **durability**, **safety** and **security**.[1] In software engineering, **dependability** is the ability to provide services that can defensibly be trusted within a time-period.[2] This may also encompass mechanisms designed to increase and maintain the dependability of a system or software.[3]

629   In summary, deciding which "ility" is more important than others must be dealt with on a case by
630   case basis. It is recommended that the "ilities" are considered at the beginning of the life-cycle of
631   a network of 'things.' Failure to do so will cause downstream problems throughout the system's
632   life-cycle, and it may continually cause contention as to why intended behaviors do not match
633   actual behaviors.

634

635 **7   Synchronization**

636 A network of 'things' is a distributed computing system. Distributed computing systems have
637 different computations and events occurring concurrently. There can be numerous computations
638 and events (e.g., data transfers) occurring in parallel.

639 This creates an interesting dilemma, similar to that in air traffic control: trying to keep all events
640 properly synchronized and executing at the precise times and in a precise order. When events
641 and computations get out of order due to delays or failures, an entire ecosystem can become
642 unbalanced and unstable.

643 IoT is no different, and possibly more complex than air traffic control. In air traffic control,
644 there is a basic global clock that does not require events be timestamped to high levels of fidelity,
645 e.g., a microsecond. Further, events are regionalized around particular airspace sectors and
646 airports.

647 There is nothing similar in IoT. Events and computations can occur anywhere, be transferred at
648 "any time", and occur at differing levels of speed and performance. The desired result is that all
649 these events and computations converge towards a single decision (output). The key concern is
650 "any time", because these transactions can take place geographically anywhere, at the
651 microsecond level, and with no clear understanding of what the clock in one geographic region
652 means with respect to the clock in another geographic region.

653 There is no trusted universal timestamping mechanism for practical use in many or most IoT
654 applications. The Global Positioning System (GPS) can provide very precise time, accurate up
655 to 100 nanoseconds with most devices. Unfortunately, GPS devices have two formidable
656 limitations for use in IoT. First, GPS requires unobstructed line of sight access to satellite
657 signals. Many IoT devices are designed to work where a GPS receiver could not receive a signal,
658 such as indoors or otherwise enclosed in walls or other obstructions. Additionally, even if an IoT
659 device is placed where satellite signal reception is available, GPS power demands are significant.
660 Many IoT devices have drastically limited battery life or power access, requiring carefully
661 planned communication schedules to minimize power usage. Adding the comparatively high-
662 power demands of GPS devices to such a system could cripple it, so in general GPS may not be
663 practical for use in many networks of things.

664 Consider a scenario where a sensor in geographic location v is supposed to release data at time x.
665 There is an aggregator in location z waiting to receive this sensor's data concurrently with
666 outputs from other sensors. Note that v and z are geographically far apart and the local time x in
667 location v does not agree, at a global level, with what time it is at z. If there existed a universal
668 timestamping mechanism, local clocks could be avoided altogether, and this problem would go
669 away. With universal timestamping, the time of every event and computation in a network of
670 'things' could be agreed upon by using a central timestamping authority that would produce
671 timestamps for all events and computations that request them. Because timing is a vital
672 component needed to trust distributed computations, such an authority would be beneficial.
673 However, such an authority does not exist [Stavrou, 2017]. Research is warranted here.

674

8   Lack of Measurement

Standards are intended to offer levels of trust, comparisons of commonality, and predictions of certainty. Standards are needed for nearly everything, but without metrics and measures, standards become more difficult to write and determine compliance against. Metrics and measures are classified in many ways.

Measurement generally allows for determination of one of two things: (1) what currently exists, and (2) what is predicted and expected in the future. The first is generally easier to measure. One example is *counting*. For example, one can count the number of coffee beans in a bag. Another approach is estimation. *Estimation* approximates what you have. By using the coffee example and having millions of beans to count, it might be easier weighing the beans and using that weight to estimate an approximate count.

Prediction is different than estimation, although estimation can be used for prediction. For example, an estimate of the current reliability of a system, given a fixed environment, context, and point in time might be 99%. Note the key word is point in time. In comparison, a prediction would say something like: based on an estimate of 99% reliability today, it is believed that the reliability will also be 99% reliable tomorrow, but after tomorrow, the reliability might change. Why? The reason is simple: As *time* moves forward, components usually wear out, thus reducing overall system reliability. Or as time moves forward, the environment may change such that the system is under less stress, thus increasing predicted reliability. In IoT, as 'things' may be swapped in and out on a quick and continual basis, predictions and estimations of an "ility" such as reliability will be difficult.

To date, there are few ways to measure IoT systems other than by *counting* 'things' or dynamic testing. Counting is a static approach. Testing is a dynamic approach when the network is executed. (Note that there are static testing approaches that do not require network execution, e.g., a walkthrough of the network architecture.) Thus, the number of 'things' in a system can be counted just like how lines of code in software can be counted, and black-box testing can be used to measure certain "ilities."

In summary, several limited recommendations have been mentioned for mitigating the current lack of measurement and metrics for IoT. To date, counting measures and dynamic approaches such as estimating reliability and performance are reasonable candidates. Static testing (e.g., code checking) can also be used to show that certain classes of IoT vulnerabilities are likely not present. IoT metrology is an open research question.

708 **9   Predictability**

709 The ability to design useful IT systems depends at a fundamental level on predictability, the
710 assurance that components will provide the resources, performance, and functions that are
711 specified when they are needed. This is hard enough to establish in a conventional system, but
712 an extensive body of knowledge in queueing theory and related subjects has been developed.
713 IoT systems will provide an even greater challenge, since more components will interact in
714 different ways, and possibly not at consistent times.

715 Two properties of IoT networks have a major impact on predictability: (1) a much larger set of
716 communication protocols may be involved in a single network, and (2) the network configuration
717 changes rapidly. Communication protocols for networks of 'things' include at least 13 data
718 links, 3 network layer routings, 5 network layer encapsulations, 6 session layers, and 2
719 management standards [Salman]. Data aggregators in the network must thus be able to
720 communicate with devices that have widely varying latency, throughput, and storage
721 characteristics. Since many small devices have limited battery life, data transmission times must
722 be rationed, so devices are not always online. For example, Bluetooth Low Energy (BLE)
723 devices can be configured to broadcast their presence for periods ranging from 0.2 seconds to
724 10.2 seconds.

725 In addition to second-by-second changes in the set of devices currently active, another issue with
726 network configuration changes stems from the embedding of computing devices with the
727 physical world. Even more than conventional systems, humans are part of IoT systems, and
728 necessarily affect the predictable availability of services, often in unexpected ways. Consider the
729 story of a driver who took advantage of a cell phone app that interacts with his vehicle's onboard
730 network to allow starting the car with the phone. Though probably not considered by the user,
731 the starting instructions are routed through the cellular network. The car owner started his car
732 with the cell phone app, then later parked the car in a mountainous area, only to discover that it
733 was impossible to re-start the car because there was no cell signal [Neumann, 2018].

734 This rather amusing story illustrates a basic predictability problem for IoT networks - node
735 location and signal strength may be constantly changing. How do you know if a constantly
736 changing network will continue to function adequately, and remain safe? Properties such as
737 performance and capacity are unavoidably affected as the configuration evolves, but you need to
738 be able to predict these to know if and how a system can be used for specific purposes.
739 Modeling and simulation become essential for understanding system behavior in a changing
740 environment, but trusting a model requires some assurance that it incorporates all features of
741 interest and accurately represents the environment. Beyond this, it must be possible to
742 adequately analyze system interactions with the physical world, including potentially rare
743 combinations of events.

744 Recommendations for design principles will evolve for this new environment but will take time
745 before users are able to trust systems composed often casually from assorted components. Here
746 again, the importance of a central theme of this document is reshown: to be able to trust a
747 system, it must be bounded, but IoT by its nature may defy any ability to bound the problem.

748

749 **10   Few IoT-specific Testing and Assurance Approaches**

750 To have any trust in networks of 'things' acting together, assurance will need to be much better
751 than it is today. A network of 'things' presents a number of testing challenges beyond those
752 encountered with conventional systems. Some of the more significant include:

753 - *Communication among large numbers of devices.* Conventional internet-based systems
754   usually include one or more servers responding to short communications from users.
755   There may be thousands of users, but the communication is typically one-to-one, with
756   possibly a few servers cooperating to produce a response to users. Networks of 'things'
757   may have several tens to hundreds of devices communicating.

758 - *Significant latency and asynchrony.* Low power devices may conserve power by
759   communicating only on a periodic basis, and it may not be possible to synchronize
760   communications.

761 - *More sources of failure.* Inexpensive, low power devices may be more likely to fail, and
762   interoperability problems may also occur among devices with slightly different protocol
763   implementations. Since the devices may have limited storage and processing power,
764   software errors in memory management or timing may be more common.

765 - *Dependencies among devices matter.* With multiple nodes involved in decisions or
766   actions, some nodes will typically require data from multiple sensors or aggregators, and
767   there may be dependencies in the order this data is sent and received. The odds of failure
768   increase rapidly as the chain of cooperating devices grows longer.

769 The concerns listed above produce a complex problem for testing and assurance, exacerbated by
770 the fact that many IoT applications may be safety critical. In these cases, the testing problem is
771 harder, but the stakes may be higher than for most testing. For essential or life-critical
772 applications, conventional testing and assurance will not be acceptable.

773 For a hypothetical example, consider a future remote health monitoring and diagnosis app, with
774 four sensors connected to two aggregators, which are connected to an e-Utility that is then
775 connected to a local communication channel, which in turn connects to the external internet, and
776 finally with a large artificial intelligence application at a central decision trigger node. While
777 99.9% reliability might seem acceptable for a $3.00 device, it will not be, if included in a critical
778 system. If correct operation depends on all 10 of these nodes, and each node is 99.9% reliable,
779 then there is nearly a 1% chance that this network of things will fail its mission, an unacceptable
780 risk for life-critical systems. Worse, this analysis has not even considered the reverse path from
781 the central node with instructions back to the originating app.

782 Basic recommendations to reduce this level of risk include redundancy among nodes, and much
783 better testing. This mean not just more of conventional test and review activities, but different
784 kinds of testing and verification. For some IoT applications, it will be necessary to meet test
785 criteria closer to what are used in applications such as telecommunications and avionics, which
786 are designed to meet requirements for failure probabilities of 10^{-5} and 10^{-9} respectively.
787 Redundancy is part of the answer, with a tradeoff that interactions among redundant nodes

788   become more critical, and the redundant node interactions are added to the already large number
789   of interacting IoT nodes.

790   One additional testing and assurance issue concerns the *testability* of IoT systems [Voas, 2018b].
791   There are various meanings of this "ility," however two that apply here are: (1) the ability of
792   testing to detect defects, and (2) the ability of testing to cover[5] (execute) portions of the system
793   using a fixed set of test cases. The reason (1) is a concern is that IoT systems may have small
794   output ranges, e.g., a system may only produce a binary output. Such systems, if very complex,
795   may inherit an ability to hide defects during testing. The reason (2) is a concern is that if high
796   levels of test coverage cannot be achieved, more portions of the overall system will go untested
797   leaving no clue as to what might happen when those portions are executed during operation.

798   The key problem for IoT testing is apparent from the test issues discussed above - huge numbers
799   of interactions among devices and connections, coupled with order dependencies. Fortunately,
800   methods based on combinatorics and design of experiments work extremely well in testing
801   complex interactions [Patil, 2015; Dhadyalla, 2014; Yang, 2013]. Covering array generation
802   algorithms compress huge numbers of input value combinations into arrays that are practical for
803   most testing, making the problem more tractable, and coverage more thorough, than would be
804   possible with traditional use case-based testing. Methods of dealing with this level of testing
805   complexity are the subject of active research [Voas, 2018b].

806

---

[5] Coverage too comes in different types, for instance the ability to execute each 'thing' once is different than executing each path
    through a system once.

807 | **11   Lack of IoT Certification Criteria**

808 Certification of a product (not processes or people) is a challenge for any hardware, software,
809 service, and hybrid systems [Voas, 1998a; Voas, 1999; Voas, 2000a; Voas, 200b; Miller, 2006;
810 Voas, 2008c; Voas, 1998b]. IoT systems are hybrids that may include services (e.g., clouds)
811 along with hardware and software.

812 If rigorous IoT certification approaches are eventually developed, they should reduce many of
813 the trust concerns in this publication. However, building certification approaches is generally
814 difficult [Voas, 1999]. One reason is that certification approaches have less efficacy unless
815 correct threat spaces and operational environments are known. Often, these are not known for
816 traditional systems, let alone for IoT systems.

817 Certification economics should also be considered, e.g., the cost to certify a 'thing' relative to the
818 value of that 'thing.' The *criteria* used during certification must be rigorous enough to be of
819 value. And a question of who performs the certification and what their qualifications are to
820 perform this work cannot be overlooked. Two other considerations are: (1) what is the impact on
821 the time-to-market of a 'thing' or network of 'things'? and (2) what is the lifespan of a 'thing' or
822 network of 'things'? These temporal questions are important because networks of 'things' along
823 with their components may have short lives that far exceed the time needed to certify.

824 Certifying 'things' as standalone entities does not solve the problem of system trust, particularly
825 for systems that operate in a world where their environment and threat space is in continual flux.

826 If 'things' have their functional and non-functional requirements defined, they can be vetted to
827 assess their ability to: (1) be integrated, (2) communicate with other 'things', (3) not create
828 conflict (e.g., no malicious output behaviors), and (4) be swapped in and out of a network of
829 'things', (e.g., when a newer or replacement 'thing' becomes available).

830 When composing 'things' into systems, special consideration must be given if all of the 'things'
831 are not certified. For example, not all 'things' in a system may have equal significance to the
832 functionality of the system. It would make sense to spend vetting resources on those that have
833 the greatest impact. Therefore, weighting the importance of each 'thing' should be considered,
834 and then decide what to certify and what to ignore based on the weightings. And if all 'things'
835 are certified, that still does not mean they will interoperate correctly in a system because the
836 environment, context, and the threat space all plays a key role in that determination.

837 And perhaps most importantly, what functional, non-functional, or negative behavior is being
838 certified for? And are forms of vetting available to do that? For example, how can a network of
839 'things' demonstrate that certain security vulnerabilities are not present?

840 In summary, limited recommendations can be considered for how to certify 'things' and systems
841 of 'things.' Software testing is a first line of defense for performing lower levels of certification,
842 however it is costly and can over estimate quality, e.g., you test a system twice and if it works,
843 potentially leading to a false assumption that the system is reliable and does not need a third test.
844 Probably a good first step here is to first define the type of quality you are concerned about. (See
845 Section 6.) From there, you can assess what can be certified in a timely manner and at what cost.

846

12   Security

848 Like traditional IT or enterprise security, IoT security is not a one-size-fits-all problem, and the
849 solutions deployed to this problem tend to only be quick fixes that push the issue down the line.
850 Instead, it should be recognized that the issue of IoT security is both multi-faceted and dependent
851 on the effort to standardize IoT security. This section walks through several of these important
852 facets, highlighting solutions that do exist and problems that remain to be solved.

853 ### 12.1   Security of 'Things'

854 Security is a concern for all 'things.' For example, sensors and their data may be tampered with,
855 stolen, deleted, dropped, or transmitted insecurely allowing it to be accessed by unauthorized
856 parties. Further, sensors may return no data, totally flawed data, partially flawed data due to
857 malicious intent. Sensors may fail completely or intermittently and may lose sensitivity or
858 calibration due to malicious tampering. Note however that building security into specific sensors
859 may not be cost effective depending on the value of a sensor or the importance of the data it
860 collects. Aggregators may contain malware affecting the correctness of their aggregated data.
861 Further, aggregators could be attacked, e.g., by denying them the ability to execute or by feeding
862 them bogus data. Communication channels are prone to malicious disturbances and interruptions.

863 The existence of counterfeit 'things in the marketplace cannot be dismissed. Unique identifiers
864 for every 'thing' would be ideal for mitigating this problem but that is not practical. Unique
865 identifiers can partially mitigate this problem by attaching Radio Frequency identifier (RFID)
866 tags to physical primitives. RFID readers that work on the same protocol as the inlay may be
867 distributed at key points throughout a network of 'things.' Readers activate a tag causing it to
868 broadcast radio waves within bandwidths reserved for RFID usage by individual governments
869 internationally. These radio waves transmit identifiers or codes that reference unique information
870 associated with the item to which the RFID inlay is attached, and in this case, the item would be
871 a physical IoT primitive.

872 The time at which computations and other events occur may also be tampered with, making it
873 unclear when events actually occurred, not by changing time (which is not possible), but by
874 changing the recorded time at which an event in the workflow is generated, or computation is
875 performed, e.g., sticking in a **delay()** function call. Malicious latency to induce delays, are
876 possible and will affect when decision triggers are able to execute.

877 Thus, networks of 'things', timing, and 'things' themselves are all vulnerable to malicious intent.

878 ### 12.2   Passwords

879 Default credentials have been a problem plaguing the security community for some time. Despite
880 the many guides that recommend users and administrators change passwords during system
881 setup, IoT devices are not designed with this standard practice in mind. In fact, most IoT devices
882 often lack intuitive user interfaces with which credentials can be changed. While some IoT
883 device passwords are documented either in user manuals or on manufacturer websites, some
884 device passwords are never documented and are unchangeable. Indeed, both scenarios can be

885   leveraged by botnets. The Mirai botnet and its variants successfully brute forced IoT device
886   default passwords to ultimately launch distributed denial of service attacks against various
887   targets [Kolias, 2017].

888   Many practitioners have proposed solutions to the problem of default credentials in IoT systems,
889   ranging from the usual recommendation to change credentials – perhaps with more user
890   awareness – to more advanced ideas like encouraging manufacturers to randomize passwords per
891   device. While not explicitly mitigating the problem of default credentials, the Manufacturer
892   Usage Description (MUD) specification [Lear, 2017] allows manufacturers to specify authorized
893   network traffic, which can reduce the damage caused by default credentials. This specification
894   employs a defense-in-depth strategy intended to address a variety of problems associated with
895   the widespread use of sensor enabled end devices such as IP cameras and smart thermostats.
896   MUD reduces the threat surface of an IoT device by explicitly restricting communications to and
897   from the IoT device to sources and destinations intended by the manufacturer. This approach
898   prevents vulnerable or insecure devices from being exploited and helps alleviate some of the
899   fallout of manufacturers leaving in default credentials.

900   **12.3 Secure Upgrade Process**

901   On a traditional personal computer, weaknesses are typically mitigated with patches and
902   upgrades to various software components, including the operating system. On established
903   systems, these updates are usually delivered via a secure process, where the computer can
904   authenticate the source pushing the patch. While parallels exist for IoT devices, very few
905   manufacturers have secure upgrade processes with which to deliver patches and updates;
906   oftentimes attackers can man-in-the-middle the traffic to push their own malicious updates to the
907   devices, thereby compromising them. Similarly, IoT devices can receive feature and
908   configuration updates, which can likewise be hijacked by attackers for malicious effect.

909   Transport standards such as HTTPS as well as existing public-key infrastructure provide
910   protections against many of the attacks that could be launched against upgrading IoT devices.
911   These standards, however, are agnostic on the implementations of the IoT architecture, and do
912   not cover all the edge cases. However, the IoT Firmware Update Architecture [Moran, 2017] --
913   recently proposed to the IETF – provides necessary details needed to implement a secure
914   firmware update architecture, including hard rules defining how device manufacturers should
915   operate. Following this emerging standard could easily mitigate many potential attack vectors
916   targeting IoT devices.

917   **12.4 Summary**

918   Addressing the security of IoT devices is a prescient issue as IoT continues to expand into daily
919   life. While security issues are widespread in IoT ecosystems, existing solutions – such as MUD
920   to remediate password weaknesses and transport standards for secure upgrades – can be
921   leveraged to boost the overall security of devices. Deploying these existing solutions can yield
922   significant impacts on the overall security without requiring significant amounts of time spent
923   researching new technologies.

924

925 **13   Reliability**

926   IoT reliability should be based on the traditional definition in [Musa, 1987]. The traditional
927   definition is simply the probability of failure-free operation of individual components, groups of
928   components, or the whole system over a bounded time interval and in a fixed environment. Note
929   that is what the informal definition of trust mentioned earlier was based on. This definition assumes
930   a static IoT system, meaning new 'things' are not continually being swapped in and out. But
931   realistically, that will not be the case since new 'things' will be added dynamically and on-the-fly,
932   either deliberately or inadvertently. Thus, the instantaneously changing nature of IoT systems will
933   induce emergent and complex chains of custody make it difficult to insure and correctly measure
934   reliability [Miller 2010; Voas 2018a]. The dynamic quality of IoT systems requires that reliability
935   be reassessed when components change and the operating environment changes.

936   Reliability is a function of context and environment. Therefore, to perform reliability
937   assessments, *a priori* knowledge of the appropriate environment and context is needed. It will
938   rarely be possible to make a claim such as: *this network of 'things' works perfectly for any*
939   *environment, context, and for any anomalous event that the system can experience.*
940   Unfortunately, wrong assumptions about environment and context will result in wrong
941   assumptions about the degree to which trust has been achieved.

942   To help distinguish the difference between context and environment, consider a car that fails
943   after a driver breaks an engine by speeding above the manufacturer's maximum expectation
944   while driving in excellent road conditions and good weather. Weather and road conditions are
945   the environment. Speeding past the manufacturer's maximum expectation is the context.
946   Violating the expected context or expected environment can both impact failure. But here, failure
947   occurred due to context.

948   The relationship between anomalous events and 'thing's is important for a variety of reasons, not
949   the least of which is the loss of ownership and control already mentioned. Assume worst case
950   scenarios from 'things' that are complete black-boxes.

951   Consider certain scenarios: (1) a 'thing' fails completely or in a manner that creates bad data that
952   infects the rest of the system, and (2) a 'thing' is fed corrupt data and you wish to know how that
953   'thing' reacts, i.e., is it resilient? Here, resilience means that the 'thing' still provides acceptable
954   behavior. These two scenarios have been referred to as "propagation across" and "propagation
955   from" [Voas, 1997]. Propagation across is the study of "garbage in garbage out." Propagation
956   across tests the strength of a component or 'thing.' Propagation from is the study of how far
957   through a system an internal failure that creates corrupt data can cascade. Possibly it propagates
958   all of the way and the system fails, or possibly the corrupted internal state of the system is not
959   severe enough to cause that. In this case, the system shows its resilience.

960   A related concern involves who is to blame when a 'thing' or network of 'things' fails? This
961   trust concern (and legal liability) becomes especially problematic when there are unplanned
962   interactions between critical and noncritical components. In discussing IoT trust, there are two
963   related questions: (1) What is the possibility of system failure? and (2) Who is liable when the
964   system fails? [Voas, 2017a]

965 Consider the first question: What is the possibility of system failure? The answer to this question
966 is very difficult to determine. A powerful technique for determining the risks of a system-level
967 failure would involve fault injection to simulate the effects of real faults as opposed to simulating
968 the faults themselves. But until these risks can be accurately and scientifically measured, there
969 likely won't be a means for probabilistically and mathematically bounding and quantifying
970 liability [Voas, 2017a].

971 Now consider the second question: Who is liable when the system fails? For any non-
972 interconnected system, the responsibility for failure lies with the developer (that is the individual,
973 individuals, company, or companies, inclusive). But for systems that are connected to other
974 systems locally and through the Internet, the answer becomes more difficult. Consider the
975 following legal opinion:

976   In case of (planned) interconnected technologies, when there is a 'malfunctioning
977   thing' it is difficult to determine the perimeter of the liability of each supplier.
978   The issue is even more complex for artificial intelligence systems involving a
979   massive amount of collected data so that it might be quite hard to determine the
980   reason why the system made a specific decision at a specific time. [Coraggio,
981   2016]

982 Interactions, both planned and spontaneous, between critical and noncritical systems create
983 significant risk and liability concerns. These interacting, dynamic, cross-domain ecosystems
984 create the potential for increased threat vectors, new vulnerabilities, and new risks.
985 Unfortunately, many of these will remain as unknown unknowns until after a failure or
986 successful attack has occurred.

987 In summary, this publication offers no unique recommendations for assessing and measuring
988 reliability. The traditional reliability measurement approaches that have been around for decades
989 are appropriate for a 'thing' and a network of 'things.' These approaches, as well as assessments
990 of resilience, should be considered throughout a system's life-cycle.

991

992 **14   Data Integrity**

993   Data is the 'blood' of any computing system including IoT systems. And if a network of 'things'
994   involves many sensors, there may be a lot of data.

995   The ability to trust data involves many factors: (1) accuracy, (2) fidelity, (3) availability, (4)
996   confidence that the data cannot be corrupted or tampered with, etc. Whether any of these is more
997   important than the other depends on the system's requirements, however with respect to a
998   network of 'things', the timeliness with which the data is transferred is of particular importance.
999   Stale, latent, and tardy data is a trust concern, and while that is not a direct problem with the
1000 "goodness" of the data itself, it is a performance concern for the mechanisms within the network
1001 of 'things' that transfer data. In short, stale, latent, and tardy data in certain situations will be no
1002 worse than no data at all.

1003 Cloud computing epitomizes the importance of trusting data. Where data resides is important.
1004 Where is the cloud? And can the data be leaked from that location? It is a tendency to think of
1005 "your data" on "your machine." But in some cases, the data is not just "yours." Leased data can
1006 originate from anywhere and from vendors at the time of their choosing and with the integrity of
1007 their choosing. Competitors can lease the same data [Miller, 2010; NIST, 2016].

1008 The production, communication, transformation, and output of large amounts of data in networks
1009 of 'things' creates various concerns related to trust. A few of these include:

1010   1. **Missing or incomplete data** How does one identify and address missing or incomplete
1011   data? Here, missing or incomplete data could originate from a variety of causes, but in
1012   IoT, it probably refers to sensor data that is not released and transferred or databases of
1013   information that are inaccessible (e.g., clouds). Each network of 'things' will need some
1014   level of resilience to be built-in to allow a potentially crippled network of 'things' to still
1015   perform even when data is missing or incomplete.

1016   2. **Data quality** How do one address data quality? To begin, a definition is needed for what
1017   data quality means for a particular system. Is it fidelity of the information, accuracy of
1018   the information, etc.? Each network of 'things' will need some description for what an
1019   acceptable level of data quality is.

1020   3. **Faulty interfaces and communication protocols** How does one identify and address
1021   faulty interfaces and communication protocols? Here, since data is the 'blood' of a
1022   network of 'things', then the interfaces and communication protocols are the veins and
1023   arteries of that system. Defective mechanisms that perform data transfer within a system
1024   if 'things' are equally as damaging to the overall trust in the data as is poor data quality,
1025   missing, and incomplete data. Therefore, trust must exist in the data transfer mechanisms.
1026   Each network of 'things' will need some level of resilience to be built in to ensure that
1027   the data moves from point A to point B in a timely manner. This solution might include
1028   fault tolerance techniques such as redundancy of the interfaces and protocols.

1029   4. **Data tampering** How does one address data tampering or even know it occurred? Rarely
1030   can tamperproof data exist if someone has malicious intent and the appropriate resources

1031   to fulfill that intent. Each network of 'things' will need some type of a reliance plan for
1032   data tampering, such as a back-up collection of the original data and in a different
1033   geographic location.

1034   5. **Data security and privacy** How secure and private is the data from delay or theft? There
1035   are a seemingly infinite number of places in the dataflow of a network of 'things' where
1036   data can be snooped by adversaries. This requires that the specification of a network of
1037   'things' have had some risk assessment that assigns weights to the value of the data if it
1038   were to be compromised. Each network of 'things' will need a data security and privacy
1039   plan.

1040   6. **Data leakage** Can data leak, and if so, would you know that it had? Assume worst case
1041   scenario where all networks of 'things' leak. While this does not directly impact the data,
1042   it may well impact the business model of the organization that relies on the system of
1043   'things.' If this is problematic, an analysis of where the leakage could originate can be
1044   performed, however this is technically difficult and costly.

1045 While conventional techniques such as error correcting codes, voting schemes and Kalman filters
1046 could be used, specific recommendations for design principles need to be determined on a case
1047 basis.
1048

1049 ## 15   Excessive Data

1050 Any network of 'things' is likely to have a dynamic and rapidly changing dataflow and
1051 workflow. There may be numerous inputs from a variety of sources such as sensors, external
1052 databases or clouds, and other external subsystems. The potential for the generation of vast
1053 amounts of data over time renders IoT systems as potential 'big data' generators. In fact, one
1054 report predicts that global data will reach 44 zettabytes (44 billion terabytes) by 2020 [Data IQ
1055 News]. (Note however there will be networks of 'things' that are not involved in receiving or
1056 generating large quantities of data, e.g., closed loop systems that have a small and specialized
1057 purpose. An example here would be a classified network that is not tethered to the Internet.)

1058 The data generated in any IoT system can be corrupted by sensors, aggregators, communications
1059 channels, and other hardware and software utilities [NIST, 2016]. Data is not only susceptible to
1060 accidental corruption and delay, but also malicious tampering, delay, and theft. As previously
1061 mention in Section 14, data is often the most important asset to be protected from a cybersecurity
1062 perspective.

1063 Each of the primitives presented in [NIST, 2016] is a potential source for a variety of classes of
1064 corrupt data. Section 13 already discussed the problems of "propagation across" and
1065 "propagation from." Although hyperbole, it is reasonable to visualize an executing network of
1066 'things' to a firework show. Different explosions occur at different times although all are in
1067 timing coordination during a show. Networks of 'things' are similar in that internal computations
1068 and the resulting data is in continuous generation until the IoT system performs an actuation or
1069 decision.

1070 The dynamic of data being created quickly and used to create new data and so on cannot be
1071 dismissed as a problem for testing and any hope of traceability and observability when an
1072 unexpected behavior occurs. Thus, the vast amount of data that can be generated by networks of
1073 'things' makes the problem of isolating and treating corrupt data extremely difficult. The
1074 difficulty pertains to the problem of identifying corrupt data and the problem of making this
1075 identification quickly enough. If such identification cannot be made for a certain system in a
1076 timely manner, then trust in that system is an unreasonable expectation [Voas, 2018b].

1077 Certain data compression, error detection and correction, cleaning, filtering and compression
1078 techniques may be useful both in increasing trust in the data and reducing its bulk for
1079 transmission and storage. No specific recommendations, however, are made.

1080

1081 **16   Speed and Performance**

1082   The speed at which computations and data generation can occur in a network of 'things' is
1083   increasing rapidly. Increased computational speed inhibits a systems' ability to log and audit any
1084   transactions as the rate of data generation exceeds the speed of storage. This situation, in turn,
1085   makes real-time forensic analysis and recovery from faults and failures more difficult as data is
1086   lost and computational deadlines become harder to meet. Consequently, there are fewer ways to
1087   "put on the brakes," undo incorrect computations, and fix internal and external data anomalies.
1088   Furthermore, computing faster to a wrong outcome offers little trust.

1089   A related problem is that of measuring the speed of any network of 'things'. Speed oriented
1090   metrics are needed for optimization, comparison between networks of 'things', and identification
1091   of slowdowns that could be due to anomalies – all of which affect trust.

1092   But there are no simple speed metrics for IoT systems and no dashboards, rules for
1093   interoperability and composability, rules of trust, established approaches to testing [Voas,
1094   2018a].

1095   Possible candidate metrics to measure speed in an IoT system include:

1096   1. Time to decision once all requisite data is presented; this is an end-to-end measure.

1097   2. Throughput speed of the underlying network,

1098   3. Weighted average of a cluster of sensor's "time to release data",

1099   4. Some linear combination of the above or other application domain specific metrics.

1100   Note here that while better performance will usually be an "ility" of desire, it makes the ability to
1101   perform forensics on system that fail much harder, particularly, for systems where some
1102   computations occur so instantaneously that there is no "after the fact" trace of them.

1103   Traditional definitions from real-time systems engineering can also be used, for example:

1104   1. **Response time**: The time between the presentation of a set of inputs to a system and the
1105   realization of the required behavior, including the availability of all associated outputs.

1106   2. **Real-time system**: A system in which logical correctness is based on both the correctness
1107   of the outputs and their timelines.

1108   3. **Hard real-time system**: A system in which failure to meet even a single deadline may lead
1109   to complete or catastrophic system failure.

1110   4. **Firm real-time system**: A system in which a few missed deadlines will not lead to total
1111   failure but missing more than a few may lead to complete or catastrophic system failure.

1112   5. **Soft real-time system**: A system in which performance is degraded but not destroyed by
1113   failure to meet response-time constraints [Laplante, 2012].

1114   These traditional measures of performance can be recommended as building blocks for next
1115   generation IoT trust metrics. For example, taking a weighted average of response times across a
1116   set of actuation and event combinations can give a "response time" for an IoT system. Once
1117   "response time" is defined, then notions of deadline satisfaction and designation of hard, firm, or
1118   soft real-time can be assigned. Furthermore, repositories of performance data for various types of
1119   IoT systems, devices and communications channels should be created for benchmarking
1120   purposes and eventual development of standards.

1121

1122 **17   Usability**

1123 One of the larger concerns in IoT trust is usability - the extent to which a product can be used by
1124 specified users to achieve specified goals with effectiveness, efficiency and satisfaction in a
1125 specified context of user - essentially, how "friendly" devices are to use and learn. This factor is
1126 an important consideration for most IT systems, but may be more of a challenge with IoT, where
1127 the user interface may be tightly constrained by limited display size and functionality, or where a
1128 device can only be controlled via remote means. User interfaces for some device classes, such as
1129 Smart Home devices, are often limited to a small set of onboard features (e.g., LED status
1130 indicators and a few buttons) and a broader set of display and control parameters accessible
1131 remotely via a computer or mobile device.   Some "smart" household items such as light bulbs
1132 or faucets, may have no direct interface on the device, and must be managed through a computer
1133 or smart phone connected wirelessly.

1134 Such limited interfaces have significant implications for user trust. How do users know what
1135 action to take to produce a desired response, and how does the device issue a confirmation that
1136 will be understood? Devices with only a small display and one or two buttons often end up
1137 requiring complex user interactions, that depend on sequences and timing of button presses or
1138 similar non-obvious actions. Consequently, many basic security functions can only be
1139 accomplished using a secondary device such as a smart phone. For example, if the IoT device
1140 has only two buttons, a password update will have to be done through the secondary device. As
1141 a result of this usability problem, users become even less likely to change default passwords,
1142 leaving the device open to attack. This is just one example of the interplay between usability and
1143 other trust factors. The following discussion illustrates some of the complex interactions
1144 between usability engineering and factors such as performance, security, and synchronization.

1145 Limited interfaces may to some extent be unavoidable with small devices but go against secure
1146 system principles harkening to Kerckhoffs' rules for crypto systems from the 19th century
1147 [Kerckhoff, 1883], and later extended for IT systems [Salzer, 1975]. Among these is the
1148 principle that a secure system must be easy to use, and not require users to remember complex
1149 steps. IoT systems run counter to this principle by their nature. Today, device makers are
1150 inventing user interfaces that often vary wildly from device to device and manufacturer to
1151 manufacturer, almost ensuring difficulty in remembering the right steps to follow for a given
1152 device.

1153 One of the challenges of designing for IoT usability is the asynchronous operation imposed by
1154 device processing and battery limitations. Since devices may only be able to communicate
1155 periodically, with possibly minutes to hours between transmissions, conditions at a given time
1156 may be different than indicated by the last data received from a device. And since decision
1157 triggers may require readings from multiple devices, it is likely that decisions may be based on at
1158 least some currently invalid values, or actions may be delayed as the system waits for updated
1159 values. In the worst case, badly-implemented IoT can "make the real world feel very broken"
1160 [Treseler, 2014], as when flipping a light switch results in nothing happening for some time as
1161 devices communicate.

1162 In efforts to reduce usability problems, manufacturers have turned to artificial intelligence to
1163 allow users to interact with their devices. One of the most popular uses of AI is for smart

1164   speakers, which allow users to simply talk to the device to control household appliances or order
1165   products. But as with much IT, building in one feature can have significant implications for
1166   others. Implementing the desirable voice-response capability requires engineering tradeoffs that
1167   imherently impact the ability to build in security. In one well-known example, a smart speaker
1168   responded to an accidental sequence of trigger words to record a conversation, then sent the
1169   recording to someone else [Soper, 2018]. Consider the functions required for building such a
1170   system. The most obvious implication is of course that the device must be listening continuously
1171   to be able to respond without a user flipping an ON switch. And since small devices don't have
1172   the processing capacity and databases required for voice recognition, data must be sent to a
1173   larger processor in a cloud or similar service. Consequently there is an always-active listening
1174   device with a connection to the internet, clearly a security risk that will be challenging to defend
1175   against. Added to this is the need to prevent the system from misinterpreting user directions that
1176   it hears (consider how difficult it is sometimes to prevent misunderstandings between two people
1177   communicating). It is easy to see how building in usability can sometimes lead to real
1178   challenges in providing effective security.

1179   One recommendation to improve usability for devices is to provide consistency among user
1180   interfaces. Standardized approaches will need to be developed, similar to what occurred for
1181   graphical user interfaces (GUI) in the 1980s-1990s. Prior to the 1980s, computer interfaces were
1182   typically limited to keyboards and text displays with some basic graphical capabilities. Today's
1183   desktop GUIs have reasonably consistent "WIMP" (windows, icons, menus, and pointers) style
1184   interfaces that behave similarly across GUIs from different vendors, such as the desktop
1185   metaphor, double-clicking to open files, and drag-and-drop functions to manipulate objects. But
1186   this standardized interface was reached only after a decade or more of conflicting design and
1187   industry standards development. A similar process will be needed for IoT but will be longer and
1188   more difficult given the wide range of device types.

1189

1190 **18   Visibility and Discoverability**

1191   More than anything else, IoT represents the merger of information and communications
1192   technology with the physical world. This is an enormous change in the way that humans relate
1193   to technology, whose full implications will not be understood for many years. As with many
1194   aspects of technology, the change has been occurring gradually for some time, but has now
1195   reached an exponential growth phase. However, by its nature this merger of information
1196   technology with the physical world is not always obvious. Mark Weiser, who coined the term
1197   Ubiquitous Computing nearly 30 years ago, said that "The most profound technologies are those
1198   that disappear. They weave themselves into the fabric of everyday life until they are
1199   indistinguishable from it" [Weiser, 1991] Today this vision is coming true, as IoT devices
1200   proliferate into every aspect of daily life. According to one study, within four years there will be
1201   more than 500 IoT devices in an average household [Gartner], so that they truly are beginning to
1202   disappear.

1203   But is this disappearance uniformly a good thing? If a technology is invisible, then users will not
1204   be aware of its presence, or what it is doing. Trust issues related to this new technology world
1205   made news when reports suggested that smart televisions were "eavesdropping" on users
1206   [Tsukayama, 2015] [Voas, 2017b]. Voice operated remote controls in smart televisions can only
1207   work if the televisions are always "listening", but the trust implications are obvious. To resolve
1208   trust concerns in cases like this, appliances need to be configurable for users to balance
1209   convenience with their personal security and privacy requirements, and device capabilities need
1210   to be visible with clear explanation of implications.

1211   A different set of trust concerns is involved with technical aspects of device discovery in
1212   networks of 'things.'   The traditional internet was built almost entirely on the TCP/IP protocol
1213   suite, with HTML for web sites running on top of TCP/IP. Standardized communication port
1214   numbers and internationally agreed web domain names enabled consistent operation regardless
1215   of the computer or router manufacturer. Smartphones added the Bluetooth protocol for devices.
1216   This structure has not extended to IoT devices, because they generally do not have the processing
1217   power to support it. Instead, a proliferation of protocol families has developed by different
1218   companies and consortia, including Bluetooth Low Energy (BLE), ZigBee, Digital Enhanced
1219   Cordless Telecommunications Ultra Low Energy (DECT ULE), and a collection of proprietary
1220   technologies for Low Power Wide Area Networks (LPWAN). These many technologies result in
1221   a vast number of possible interactions among various versions of software and hardware from
1222   many different sources.

1223   Most computer users are familiar with problems that arise when some business application or
1224   other software will not run because other software was changed on the system, and the two
1225   packages are no longer compatible. At least with PCs and mainframes a person generally has a
1226   good idea of what is running on the systems. With 500 IoT devices in a home, will the
1227   homeowner even know where the devices are located? How do devices make their presence
1228   known, with multiple protocols? It may not be clear from day to day what devices are on a
1229   network, or where they are, much less how they are interacting.

1230   Device discovery is a complex problem for networks of things [Bello 2017; Sunthanlap 2018],
1231   but the general problem of discovery within networks has been studied for decades. There are
1232   generally two approaches:

1233   ***Centralized***: Nodes register with a central controller when they are brought into a network. The
1234   controller manages a database of currently available devices, and periodically sends out heartbeat
1235   messages to ensure devices are available, dropping from the database any that don't respond.

1236   ***Distributed***: In this case, devices conduct a search for partner devices with the necessary
1237   features, by broadcasting to the local network. This approach avoids the need for a central
1238   controller, providing flexibility and scalability.

1239   Scalability requirements for networks of hundreds of things often lead to implementing the
1240   distributed approach, but trust issues have enormous implications for device discovery in a large
1241   network. Without sophisticated cryptographically-based authentication mechanisms, it becomes
1242   very difficult to ensure trusted operation in a network. For example, it has been shown that
1243   malware installed on a smartphone can open paths to other IoT devices, leaving the home
1244   network fully vulnerable to attack [Sivaraman 2016]. This is possible primarily because many
1245   IoT devices have little or no authentication, often due to the resource constraints described
1246   earlier.

1247   Discoverability of IoT devices is thus a key problem for trust. Its dimensions include human
1248   factors, such as users trust in behavior of devices such as the smart TV example, and technical
1249   issues of authentication among devices. Solutions will require adoption of some common
1250   protocols, which may take years for development of consensus standards, or emergence of *de*
1251   *facto* proprietary standards. In many cases there will also be organizational challenges, since
1252   different kinds of devices may be installed by different departments. Organizations will need to
1253   know what devices are present, to manage security, or even just to avoid duplication of effort.
1254   This need can be addressed with audit tools that can identify and catalog devices on the network,
1255   reducing dependence on user cooperation but requiring trust in the audit tools.

1256

1257

19   Summary

1258 This publication has enumerated 17 technical trust concerns for any IoT system based on the
1259 primitives presented in [NIST, 2016]. These systems have significant differences with traditional
1260 IT systems, such as much smaller size and limited performance, larger and more diverse
1261 networks, minimal or no user interface, lack of consistent access to reliable power and
1262 communications, and many others. These differences necessitate new approaches to planning
1263 and design. An essential aspect of developing these new systems is understanding the ways in
1264 which their characteristics can affect user trust and avoiding a "business as usual" approach that
1265 might be doomed to failure in the new world of IoT.

1266 For each of the technical concerns, this publication introduced and defined the trust issues,
1267 pointed out how they differ for IoT as compared with traditional IT systems, gave examples of
1268 their effect in various IoT applications, and when appropriate, outlined solutions to dealing with
1269 the trust issues. Some of these recommendations apply not only to IoT systems but to other
1270 traditional IT systems as well. For some of the trust issues, IoT introduces complications that
1271 defy easy answers in the current level of development. These are noted as requiring research or
1272 industry consensus on solutions. This document thus offers an additional benefit of providing
1273 guidance towards a roadmap on needed standards efforts or research into how to better trust IoT
1274 systems.

1275   **Appendix A—Insurability and Risk Measurement**

1276   IoT trust issues truly come to the fore in assessing the impact of this new technology on
1277   insurability and risk management, because insurance requires that risk be measured and
1278   quantified. In this area, the emergence of IoT can have significant tradeoffs - networks of
1279   'things' can make it easier to estimate risk for the physical systems in which devices are
1280   embedded but estimating risk for the device networks themselves may be much more difficult
1281   than for conventional IT systems.

1282   Cars, homes, and factories with embedded sensors provide more data than ever, making it
1283   possible to estimate their risks more precisely, a huge benefit for insurers [Forbes, 2016]. For
1284   example, auto insurance companies have begun offering lower rates for drivers who install
1285   tracking devices in their vehicles, to report where, how, and how fast they drive. Depending on a
1286   user's privacy expectations, there are obvious trust issues, and the legal aspects of employers
1287   installing such devices to monitor employee driving are just now being developed
1288   [Grossenbacher, 2018]. Additionally, an often, neglected aspect of such devices is the possible
1289   tradeoff between reducing risk by measuring the physical world, such as with driving, and
1290   potential increased risk from a complex network of things being introduced into a vehicle or
1291   other life-critical system. Already there have been claims that vehicle tracking devices have
1292   interfered with vehicle electronics, possibly leading to dangerous situations [Neilson, 2014].
1293   Examples include claims of losing headlights and tail lights unexpectedly, and complete
1294   shutdown of the vehicle [Horcher, 2014], as a result of unexpected interactions between the
1295   vehicle monitor and other components of the car's network of things.

1296   In addition to estimating the risk, and thus insurability, of systems with embedded IoT devices,
1297   cybersecurity risks may become much harder to measure. Quantifying potential vulnerability
1298   even for conventional client-server systems, such as e-commerce, is not well understood, and
1299   reports of data loss are common. As a result, insurance against cybersecurity attacks is
1300   expensive - a $10M policy can cost $200,000 per year, because of the risk [Wall Street Journal,
1301   2018]. It will be much more difficult to measure risk for IoT networks of thousands of
1302   interacting devices than it is even for a corporate system made up of a few hundred servers and
1303   several thousand client nodes. IoT interactions are significantly more varied and more numerous
1304   than standard client-server architectures. Risk estimation for secure systems requires
1305   measurement of a *work factor*, the time and resource cost of defeating a security measure. The
1306   same principle has been applied to vaults and safes long before the arrival of IT systems - the
1307   cost of defeating system security must be much higher than the value of the assets protected, so
1308   that attackers have no motivation to attempt to break in. The problem for networks of things is
1309   that there are few good measures of the work factor involved in breaking into these systems.
1310   They are not only new technology, but they have vast differences depending on where they are
1311   applied, and it is difficult to evaluate their defenses.

1312   From a protection cost standpoint, IoT systems also have a huge negative tradeoff - the typical
1313   processor and memory resource limitations of the devices make them easier to compromise,
1314   while at the same time they may have data as sensitive as what's on a typical PC, or in extreme
1315   cases may present risks to life and health. Implantable medical devices can be much harder to
1316   secure than a home PC, but the risks are obviously much greater [Newman 2017; Rushanan,
1317   2014]. Determining the work factor in breaking security of such devices and "body area

33

1318   networks" is an unsolved problem. A basic goal may be to ensure that life-critical IoT devices
1319   adhere to sound standards for secure development [Haigh, 2015], but estimating risk for such
1320   systems is likely to remain a challenge.

1321   To complicate matters further, IoT systems often provide functions that may inspire *too much*
1322   *trust* from users. Drivers who placed unwarranted trust in vehicle autonomy have already been
1323   involved in fatal crashes, with suggestions that they were inattentive and believed the car could
1324   successfully avoid any obstacle [Siddiqui 2017]. Establishing the *right level of trust* for users
1325   will likely be a human factor challenge with IoT systems for many years to come.

1326   No specific recommendations are made here. It is inevitable that insurers and systems engineers
1327   will eventually develop appropriate risk measures and mitigation strategies for IoT systems.

1328

1329   **Appendix B—Regulatory Oversight and Governance**

1330   Regulations have the power to significantly shape consumer interaction with technologies.
1331   Consider motor vehicles, whose safety is regulated by the National Highway Traffic Safety
1332   Administration (NHTSA) [NHTSA, 2018]. NHTSA enforces the Federal Motor Vehicle Safety
1333   Standards which specify minimum safety compliance regulations for motor vehicles to meet;
1334   notable stipulations include requiring seatbelts in all vehicles, which can help reduce fatalities in
1335   the case of vehicular accidents. NHTSA likewise licenses vehicle manufacturers – helping
1336   regulate the supply of vehicles that consumers can buy – and also provides access to a safety
1337   rating system that consumers can consult. Multiple studies have shown the potential for
1338   regulations to continue to increase the safety of motor vehicles (e.g., [Neely, 2009]).

1339   Regulatory oversight and governance have been established in most domains for safety critical
1340   systems. However, there is no parallel to the NHTSA for IoT systems:

1341   1. There are no regulations on the security of IoT devices.
1342   2. There is no oversight on the licensing of IoT device manufacturers.
1343   3. There are no governing authorities evaluating the security of IoT devices.

1344   These problems are compounded due to the economies behind IoT: the barrier to entry to
1345   constructing an IoT device is low, meaning that the market contains many different devices and
1346   models from many different manufacturers, with very few authoritative bodies attesting to the
1347   security of any of these devices. While these problems extend into the traditional computing
1348   market – i.e., laptops and personal computers – the market mechanics have since driven most
1349   products towards consolidated products and features, making it easier for consumers to evaluate
1350   and understand the security offered by the devices and manufacturers.

1351   Nonetheless, while there is no central entity regulating the security of IoT devices, recent
1352   progress has been seen as regulatory participants consider how they want to approach this
1353   complex problem. As an example, the Internet of Things Cybersecurity Improvement Act
1354   [Weaver, 2017] was introduced in 2017 with the goal of setting standards for IoT devices
1355   specifically installed in government networks. The bill contains several important stipulations,
1356   including requiring devices to abandon fixed, default passwords and that devices must not have
1357   any known vulnerabilities. The act also relaxes several other acts that could be used to prosecute
1358   security researchers looking to test the safety of these devices.

1359   The mandates of several agencies border with the IoT security space. A good example of this is
1360   the Federal Trade Commission (FTC). In January 2018, the VTech Electronics agreed to settle
1361   charges by the FTC that they violated not a security law, but rather U.S. children's privacy law,
1362   collecting private information from children, not obtaining parental consent, and failing to take
1363   reasonable steps to secure the data [Federal Trade Commission, 2018]. The key phrase is that last
1364   point: VTech's products were Internet connected toys – i.e. IoT devices – which collected
1365   personal information, and due to security risks in how these devices handled and managed data,
1366   the company was fined. This case shows that if IoT devices don't have reasonable security, a
1367   manufacturer may be held liable.

1368   The U.S. Consumer Product Safety Commission has called for more collaboration between
1369   lawyers and experts in the area [American Bar Association, 2017]. Outside of the U.S., the
1370   European Union Agency for Network and Information Security (ENISA) has published
1371   recommended security guidelines for IoT [ENISA, 2017]. As more calls for security and
1372   recommendations occur, standardization and regulation may follow, increasing the security and
1373   safety of deployed IoT systems.

1374   Regulations offer a serious means with which can help increase the security and safety of IoT
1375   systems, as evidenced by their successes in other industries such as vehicle manufacturing.
1376   While some improvements have been noticed as some agencies and organizations attempt to
1377   wield influence in IoT regulation, it has not been seen where any one central organization
1378   mandates rules regarding the use and development of IoT systems. Such an organization could
1379   have significant positive impact on the security and safety of IoT systems and consumers' lives.

1380

1381   **Appendix C—Six Trustworthiness Elements in NIST SP 800-183**

1382   Six trustworthiness elements are listed in Section 3 of NIST SP 800-183. The verbatim text for
1383   those six is given here, and note that NoT stands for network of 'things':

1384   **[begin verbatim text]**

1385   To complete this model, we define six elements: *environment, cost, geographic location, owner,*
1386   *Device_ID,* and *snapshot,* that although are not primitives, are key players in trusting NoTs.
1387   These elements play a major role in fostering the degree of trustworthiness[6] that a specific NoT
1388   can provide.

1389   1. **Environment** – The universe that all primitives in a specific NoT operate in; this is
1390   essentially the *operational profile* of a NoT. The environment is particularly
1391   important to the sensor and aggregator primitives since it offers context to them. An
1392   analogy is the various weather profiles that an aircraft operates in or a particular
1393   factory setting that a NoT operates in. This will likely be difficult to correctly define.

1394   2. **Cost** – The expenses, in terms of time and money, that a specific NoT incurs in terms
1395   of the non-mitigated reliability and security risks; additionally, the costs associated
1396   with each of the primitive components needed to build and operate a NoT. Cost is an
1397   estimation or prediction that can be measured or approximated. Cost drives the design
1398   decisions in building a NoT.

1399   3. **Geographic location** – Physical place where a sensor or *e*Utility operates in, e.g.,
1400   using RFID to decide where a 'thing' actually resides. Note that the operating
1401   location may change over time. Note that a sensor's or *e*Utility's geographic location
1402   along with communication channel reliability and data security may affect the
1403   dataflow throughout a NoT's workflow in a timely manner. Geographic location
1404   determinations may sometimes not be possible. If not possible, the data should be
1405   suspect.

1406   4. **Owner** - Person or Organization that owns a particular sensor, communication
1407   channel, aggregator, decision trigger, or *e*Utility. There can be multiple owners for
1408   any of these five. Note that owners may have nefarious intentions that affect overall
1409   trust. Note further that owners may remain anonymous. Note that there is also a role
1410   for an **operator**; for simplicity, we roll up that role into the owner element.

1411   5. **Device_ID** – A unique identifier for a particular sensor, communication channel,
1412   aggregator, decision trigger, or *e*Utility. Further, a Device_ID may be the only sensor
1413   data transmitted. This will typically originate from the manufacturer of the entity, but

---

[6] *Trustworthiness* includes attributes such as security, privacy, reliability, safety, availability, and performance, to name a few.

1414   it could be modified or forged. This can be accomplished using RFID[7] for physical
1415   primitives.

1416   6. **Snapshot** – an instant in time. Basic properties, assumptions, and general statements
1417   about snapshot include:

1418   a. Because a NoT is a distributed system, different events, data transfers, and
1419   computations occur at different snapshots.

1420   b. Snapshots may be aligned to a clock synchronized within their own network
1421   [NIST 2015]. A global clock may be too burdensome for sensor networks that
1422   operate in the wild. Others, however, argue in favor of a global clock [Li
1423   2004]. This publication does not endorse either scheme at the time of this
1424   writing.

1425   c. Data, without some "agreed upon" time stamping mechanism, is of limited or
1426   reduced value.

1427   d. NoTs may affect business performance – sensing, communicating, and
1428   computing can speed-up or slow-down a NoT's workflow and therefore affect
1429   the "perceived" performance of the environment it operates in or controls.

1430   e. Snapshots maybe tampered with, making it unclear when events actually
1431   occurred, not by changing time (which is not possible), but by changing the
1432   recorded time at which an event in the workflow is generated, or computation
1433   is performed, e.g., sticking in a **delay()** function call.

1434   f. Malicious latency to induce delays, are possible and will affect when decision
1435   triggers are able to execute.

1436   g. Reliability and performance of a NoT may be highly based on (e) and (f).

1437   **[end verbatim text]**

1438   This publication has taken Section 3 from NIST SP 800-183 and expanded into a richer
1439   discussion as to why trusting IoT products and services is difficult. This document has derived
1440   17 new technical trust concerns from the six elements in NIST SP 800-183. For example, the
1441   snapshot element briefly mentioned in NIST SP 800-183 is discussed in detail in Section 7
1442   concerning a lack of precise timestamps.

---

[7] RFID readers that work on the same protocol as the inlay may be distributed at key points throughout a NoT. Readers activate
   the tag causing it to broadcast radio waves within bandwidths reserved for RFID usage by individual governments
   internationally. These radio waves transmit identifiers or codes that reference unique information associated with the item to
   which the RFID inlay is attached, and in this case, the item would be a primitive.

1443   **Appendix D—References**

1444   **[American Bar Association, 2017]** American Bar Association. Consumer Product Safety
1445   Administration seeks collaboration in managing internet of things. May 2017.
1446   https://www.americanbar.org/news/abanews/aba-news-
1447   archives/2017/05/consumer_productsaf.html Accessed 7/21/2018

1448   **[Ashton, 2009]** Ashton, K. (22 June 2009). *"That 'Internet of Things' Thing"*. *Retrieved 9 May*
1449   *2017* http://www.rfidjournal.com/articles/view?4986

1450   **[BBC, 2016]** *"Peter Day's World of Business"*. *BBC World Service. BBC. Retrieved 4 October*
1451   *2016* http://downloads.bbc.co.uk/podcasts/radio/worldbiz/worldbiz_20150319-0730a.mp3

1452   **[Bello, 2017]** Bello, O., Zeadally, S., & Badra, M. (2017). Network layer inter-operation of
1453   Device-to-Device communication technologies in Internet of Things (IoT). *Ad Hoc Networks*,
1454   *57*, 52-62.

1455   **[Columbus, 2017]** Columbus, Louis, Forbes, "Internet of Things Market to Reach $267B By
1456   2020", 1/29/17, https://www.forbes.com/sites/louiscolumbus/2017/01/29/internet-of-things-
1457   market-to-reach-267b-by-2020/#f2ddc5609bd6 (retrieved 1/5/2018).

1458   **[Coraggio, 2016]** G. Coraggio, "The Internet of Things and its Legal Dilemmas," VC Experts
1459   Blog, 15 Dec. 2016; blog.vcexperts .com/2016/12/15/the-internet-of -things-and-its-legal-
1460   dilemmas.

1461   **[Data IQ News]** DataIQ News, "Big data to turn 'mega' as capacity will hot 44 zettabytes by
1462   2020", http://www.dataiq.co.uk/news/20140410/big-data-turn-mega-capacity-will-hit-44-
1463   zettabytes-2020, Oct. 2014.

1464   **[Dhadyalla, 2014]** G. Dhadyalla, N. Kumari, and T. Snell, "Combinatorial Testing for an
1465   Automotive Hybrid Electric Vehicle Control System: A Case Study," Proc. IEEE 7th Int'l Conf.
1466   Software Testing, Verification and Validation Workshops (ICSTW 14), 2014, pp. 51–57.

1467   **[ENISA, 2017]** European Union Agency for Network and Information Security. Baseline
1468   Security Recommendations for IoT. November 2017.
1469   https://www.enisa.europa.eu/publications/baseline-security-recommendations-for-iot Accessed
1470   7/21/2018

1471   **[Federal Trade Commission, 2018]** Federal Trade Commission. Electronic Toy Maker VTech
1472   Settles FTC Allegations That it Violated Children's Privacy Law and the FTC Act. January
1473   2018. https://www.ftc.gov/news-events/press-releases/2018/01/electronic-toy-maker-vtech-
1474   settles-ftc-allegations-it-violated Accessed 7/21/2018

1475   **[Forbes, 2016]** Forbes. https://www.forbes.com/sites/robertreiss/2016/02/01/5-ways-the-iot-will-
1476   transform-the-insurance-industry/

1477   **[Gartner]** Gartner. http://www.gartner.com/newsroom/id/2839717

1478   **[Grossenbacher, 2016]** K. Grossenbacher, The Legality of Tracking Employees by GPS.
1479   https://www.laborandemploymentlawcounsel.com/2016/01/the-legality-of-tracking-employees-
1480   by-gps/

1481   **[Horcher, 2014]** G. Horcher, Concerns with insurance devices that monitor for safe-driver
1482   discounts, Atlanta Journal Constitution, 25 Nov 2014.

1483   **[Kerckhoffs, 1883]** Auguste Kerckhoffs, "La cryptographie militaire" *Journal des sciences*
1484   *militaires*, vol. IX, pp. 5–83, January 1883, pp. 161–191, February 1883.
1485   https://en.wikipedia.org/wiki/Kerckhoffs%27s_principle

1486   **[Kolias, 2017]** Kolias, C., Kambourakis, G., Stavrou, A., & Voas, J. (2017). DDoS in the IoT:
1487   Mirai and other botnets. *Computer*, *50*(7), 80-84.

1488   **[Landwehr, 2015]** Haigh T, Landwehr C. Building code for medical device software security.
1489   IEEE Cybersecurity. 2015 May.

1490   **[Laplante, 2012]** Phillip A. Laplante and Seppo J. Ovaska, Real-Time Systems Design and
1491   Analysis, Fourth Edition, John Wiley & Sons/IEEE Press, 2012.

1492   **[Lear, 2017]** Lear, E., R. Droms, and D. Romascanu. "Manufacturer Usage Description
1493   Specification." IETF draft (2017).

1494   **[Miller, 2006]** K. Miller and J. Voas, "Software Certification Services: Encouraging Trust and
1495   Reasonable Expectations", *IEEE IT Professional*, 8(5): 39-44, September 2006.

1496   **[Miller, 2010]** Keith W. Miller, Jeffrey Voas and Phil Laplante, "In Trust We Trust," IEEE
1497   Computer, October 2010, pp. 91-93.

1498   **[Moran, 2017]** Moran, B.; Meriac, M.; Tschofenig, H.: A Firmware Update Architecture for
1499   Internet of Things Devices, https://tools.ietf.org/id/draft-moran-suit-architecture-00.html, 2017.

1500   **[Musa, 1987]** J. Musa, A. Iannino, and K. Okumoto, Software Reliability: Measurement,
1501   Prediction, Application, McGraw-Hill, 1987.

1502   **[Neeley, 2009]** Neeley, G. W., & Richardson Jr, L. E. (2009). The effect of state regulations on
1503   truck-crash fatalities. *American journal of public health*, *99*(3), 408-415.

1504   **[Neilson, 2014]** Neilson, Insurance Tracking Device Blamed for Car Damage.
1505   https://www.programbusiness.com/News/Insurance-Tracking-Device-Blamed-for-Car-Damage,
1506   21 Apr 2014.

1507   **[Neumann, 2018]** P.G. Neumann, Risks Forum, June 11, 2018

1508   **[Newman, 2017]** Newman, L. H. (2017). Medical devices are the next security nightmare.
1509   *WIRED. Np*

1510 **[NHTSA, 2018]** National Highway Traffic Safety Administration. https://www.nhtsa.gov/.
1511 Accessed 7/20/2018.

1512 **[NIST, 2016]** NIST SP 800-183, "Networks of 'Things'", J. Voas, 2016.

1513 **[Patil, 2015]** A.H. Patil, N. Goveas, and K. Rangarajan, "Test Suite Design Methodology Using
1514 Combinatorial Approach for Internet of Things Operating Systems," *J. Software*
1515 *Eng.Applications*, vol. 8, no. 7, 2015, p. 303.

1516 **[Rushanan, 2014]** Rushanan, M., Rubin, A. D., Kune, D. F., & Swanson, C. M. SoK: Security
1517 and privacy in implantable medical devices and body area networks. In *Security and Privacy*
1518 *(SP), 2014 IEEE Symposium on* (pp. 524-539). IEEE.

1519 **[Salman]** T. Salman, Internet of Things Protocols. https://www.cse.wustl.edu/~jain/cse570-
1520 15/ftp/iot_prot/

1521 **[Salzer, 1975]** Saltzer, J. H., & Schroeder, M. D. (1975). The protection of information in
1522 computer systems. *Proceedings of the IEEE*, *63*(9), 1278-1308.

1523 **[Siddiqui, 2018]** F. Siddiqui, M. Laris, Self-driving Uber vehicle strikes and kills pedestrian,
1524 Washington Post, 19 Mar 2018, https://www.washingtonpost.com/news/dr-
1525 gridlock/wp/2018/03/19/uber-halts-autonomous-vehicle-testing-after-a-pedestrian-is-struck/

1526 **[Sivaraman, 2016]** Sivaraman, V., Chan, D., Earl, D., & Boreli, R. (2016, July). Smart-phones
1527 attacking smart-homes. In *Proceedings of the 9th ACM Conference on Security & Privacy in*
1528 *Wireless and Mobile Networks* (pp. 195-200). ACM.

1529 **[Stavrou, 2017]** Angelos Stavrou; Jeffrey Voas, Verified Time, *IEEE Computer*, Year:2017,
1530 Volume: 50, Issue: 3

1531 **[Soper 2018]** S. Soper, This is how Alexa Can Record Private Conversations,
1532 https://www.bloomberg.com/news/articles/2018-05-24/amazon-s-alexa-eavesdropped-and-
1533 shared-the-conversation-report

1534 **[Sunthonlap, 2018]** Sunthonlap, J., Nguyen, P., Wang, H., Pourhomanyoun, M., Zhu, Y., & Ye,
1535 Z. (2018, March). SAND: A Social-Aware and Distributed Scheme for Device Discovery in the
1536 Internet of Things. In *2018 International Conference on Computing, Networking and*
1537 *Communications (ICNC)* (pp. 38-42). IEEE.

1538 **[Treseler, 2014]** M. Treseler, How is UX for IoT Different?
1539 http://radar.oreilly.com/2014/11/how-is-ux-for-iot-different.html

1540 **[Tsukayama, 2015]** H. Tsukayama, Samsung: Our televisions aren't secretly eavesdropping on
1541 you, https://www.washingtonpost.com/news/the-switch/wp/2015/02/10/samsung-our-televisions-
1542 arent-secretly-eavesdropping-on-you/?noredirect=on&utm_term=.5322af153a88

1543 **[Voas, 1996]** J. Voas, F. Charron & K. Miller. "Tolerant Software Interfaces: Can COTS-based
1544 Systems be Trusted Without Them?" *Proceedings of the 15ᵗʰ International Conference on*

1545 *Computer Safety, Reliability and Security (SAFECOMP '96)*, Springer-Verlag, p. 126-135,
1546 October 1996, Vienna, Austria.

1547 **[Voas, 1997]** J. Voas. "Error Propagation Analysis for COTS Systems," *IEEE Computing and*
1548 *Control Engineering Journal*, 8(6): 269-272, December 1997.

1549 **[Voas, 1998a]** J. Voas. "Certifying Off-the-Shelf Software Components," *IEEE Computer*,
1550 31(6): 53-59, June 1998. (Translated into Japanese and reprinted in Nikkei Computer magazine)

1551 **[Voas, 1998b]** J. Voas. "The Software Quality Certification Triangle," *Crosstalk*, 11(11): 12-14,
1552 November 1998.

1553 **[Voas, 1999]** J. Voas. "Certifying Software for High Assurance Environments," *IEEE Software*,
1554 16(4): 48-54, July 1999.

1555 **[Voas, 2000a]** J. Voas and J. Payne. "Dependability Certification of Software Components,"
1556 *Journal of Systems and Software*, Volume 52, p. 165-172, 2000.

1557 **[Voas, 2000b]** J. Voas. "Toward a Usage-Based Software Certification Process," *IEEE*
1558 *Computer*, 33(8): 32-37, August 2000.

1559 **[Voas, 2004]** J. Voas, "Software's Secret Sauce: the `ilities," Quality Time Column, *IEEE*
1560 *Software*, 21(6): 2-3, November 2004.

1561 **[Voas, 2015]** J. Voas and G. Hurlburt, "Third Party Software's Trust Quagmire", IEEE
1562 *Computer*, December 2015.

1563 **[Voas, 2017a]** J. Voas and P. Laplante, The IoT Blame Game, *IEEE Computer*, Year:2017,
1564 Volume: 50, Issue: 6

1565 **[Voas, 2017b]** H. Chung, M. Iorga, J. Voas, "Alexa, Can I Trust You?", *IEEE Computer*,
1566 September 2017

1567 **[Voas, 2018a]** J. Voas, R. Kuhn, and P. Laplante "IoT Metrology", *IEEE IT Pro*, May 2018

1568 **[Voas, 2018b]** Voas, J., Kuhn, R., & Laplante, P. (2018, March). Testing IoT Systems. In
1569 *Service-Oriented System Engineering (SOSE), 2018 IEEE Symposium on* (pp. 48-52). IEEE.

1570 **[Voas, 2018c]** J. Voas and P. Laplante, "IoT's Certification Quagmire", *IEEE Computer*, April
1571 2018

1572 **[Wall Street Journal, 2018]** Wall Street Journal. https://www.wsj.com/articles/ransom-
1573 demands-and-frozen-computers-hackers-hit-towns-across-the-u-s-1529838001

1574 **[Weaver, 2017]** Weaver, Nicholas. The Internet of Things Cybersecurity Improvement Act: A
1575 Good Start on IoT Security. August 2017. https://www.lawfareblog.com/internet-things-
1576 cybersecurity-improvement-act-good-start-iot-security Accessed 7/21/2018

1577   **[Weiser, 1991]** Weiser, M. The Computer for the 21st Century. *Scientific American, 265*(3), 94-
1578   105.

1579   **[Yang, 2013]** Yang, J., Zhang, H., & Fu, J. (2013, August). A fuzzing framework based on
1580   symbolic execution and combinatorial testing. In *Green Computing and Communications*
1581   *(GreenCom), 2013 IEEE and Internet of Things (iThings/CPSCom), IEEE International*
1582   *Conference on and IEEE Cyber, Physical and Social Computing* (pp. 2076-2080). IEEE.

1583

1584	**Appendix E—Abbreviations**	
1585	AI	Artificial Intelligence
1586	BBC	British Broadcasting Corporation
1587	BLE	Bluetooth Low Energy
1588	COTS	Commercial Off-the-Shelf
1589	DECT ULE	Digital Enhanced Cordless Telecommunications Ultra Low Energy
1590	ENISA	European Union Agency for Network and Information Security
1591	FTC	Federal Trade Commission
1592	GPS	Global Positioning System
1593	HTML	Hypertext Markup Language
1594	HTTPS	Hypertext Transfers Protocol Secure
1595	IETF	Internet Engineering Task Force
1596	IIOT	Industrial Internet of Things
1597	IoT	Internet of Things
1598	IT	Information Technology
1599	LPWAN	Low Power Wide Area Network
1600	MUD	Manufacturer Usage Description
1601	NHTSA	National Highway Traffic Safety Administration
1602	NIST	National Institute of Standards and Technology
1603	NoT	Network of Things
1604	PC	Personal Computer
1605	RFID	Radio Frequency identification
1606	SLOC	Source Lines of Code
1607	TCP/IP	Transmission Control Protocol / Internet Protocol